PRAISE FOR

Wake Up, Maggie!
Go Away, Mom!

A Memoir In Two Voices

"Carol and her daughter Maggie share their combined story in raw and unflinching journal entries from the end of Maggie's high school years to the start of college. We learn how they experience the same events from their different perspectives, especially fights over the internet, and we read what each person is struggling with in their individual lives—loneliness, friends, love interest—and how that affects their relationship. I was immersed in this story as someone who has sent her children out into the world and was brought back to how sad I was when my daughters left. The events and emotions were familiar and validating, especially the love between mother and daughter. If you've said goodbye to a child or are anticipating it, this story will resonate with you. Even when we feel we are alone, we are in good company."

—Morgan Baker, author of *Emptying the Nest: Getting Better at Goodbyes*

Wake Up, Maggie!
Go Away, Mom!

A Memoir In Two Voices

CAROL WEIS

MARGARET HENLEY

Heliotrope Books
New York

A version of Carol's entry on page 198 first appeared in *Scary Mommy* on June 11, 2015.

An early version of the Introduction, plus a few entries, first appeared in the Literary Reflections column of the March 2006 issue of *Literary Mama*.

The poem, Like An Old Lover, also appeared in July 2005 issue of *Literary Mama*.

Cover photo by Isabella Barrios; gratitude to model Elyse Tomlet
Cover design by Carol Weis and Margaret Henley with Heliotrope Books
Designed and typeset by Heliotrope Books

Also by Carol Weis:

When the Cows Got Loose
Divorce Papers
Stumbling Home

Table of Contents

For Wonton and Wasabi,
the sweetest kitties
imaginable

Author's Note

We hope you enjoy the two sides of our story and that it helps you in some small way. A few readers may have different recollections of certain events we depict in our memoir. We've also changed the names of a number of people we've written about.

And to clear up any confusion while reading this memoir, I refer to my picture book, *When the Cows Got Loose*, as "The Day the Cows Got Loose," the working title I used before the book was published. The same with *Divorce Papers*.

Introduction

"Life is a balance between holding on and letting go."
—Rumi

Teenagers: The Reason Some Animals Eat Their Young.
—Words on old slogan button

CAROL

Letting go—whoever thinks about this part of parenting? It's something we all wrestle with and are often pushed to do. It certainly wasn't what came to mind when I decided it was time to have a baby. All I knew, the alarm on my biological clock was constantly buzzing, with no snooze button to shut it off. We tried for a solid month and nine months later, Maggie was born. I was 36, which meant she entered adolescence at the same time my body dipped into menopause. Though a single mom and teen, the Gilmore Girls we weren't. And this will come as no surprise—teenage girls and menopausal moms don't mix. What I never imagined was how hard it would be to let go of her. After all, when she was five, I gave up alcohol and her dad moved out four months later, as I started on my journey of recovery. I went back to school, got my Master's and began a life as a writer.

The idea for this project came to me when Maggie was 15. We were in the midst of the struggle many moms go through with their teenage daughters—trying to renegotiate our relationship, while attempting to let go of our old way of relating. And because Maggie and I were so close for so many years, her need to pull away and define herself apart from me was strong. The only way I knew to counteract the pain of my daughter's withdrawal and her years of individuation—to keep us connected in some way—was to write about what was going on, by keeping parallel journals.

When I initially mentioned the project to her, she thought it was a good idea. "That's cool," she said. I was pleased and somewhat surprised. We spoke of purchasing special journals, something that each of us would feel compelled to write in. But with schoolwork, friends, and drama club demanding much of her time, it wasn't surprising when she abandoned her initial enthusiasm for the venture. So I decided to let it be.

Then in April of that year, after a major argument over Internet access, I thought some retail therapy might heal the angst we were feeling, so we headed to one our favorite bookstores. Without saying a word, while standing in the checkout line with me, Maggie walked over to the journal section and picked out her favorite, a purple volume with one of Monet's *Water Lilies* floating across the cover. She persuaded me to choose one with the Eiffel Tower adorning its jacket and our journal project was born. After climbing into our beds that night, we made our first entries.

Starting out, we negotiated how we would proceed and decided to write at least two days a week. As we went along, we found it wasn't always possible, though many times we wrote more. I knew if I wanted to make this project work, I would need to be flexible. Maggie didn't want me to influence her or try to control what or how she wrote, so I assured her she could chronicle whatever she wanted, no holds barred. She agreed that I could occasionally oversee when we wrote in our journals. For that matter, Maggie never initiated our journaling on any given night during the entire endeavor.

Sometimes we agreed to write on a certain night and then wouldn't. By the time we crawled into our beds, which is when we did most of our journaling, one or both of us were too tired or would just forget to write. Sometimes days went by without writing a word. To get through this project, I knew I had to go with the flow, which wasn't always easy for me to do. I had to let this journal project take on its own life and let it unfold in its own way.

The most painful part of the endeavor was transcribing Maggie's entries. I was brought to tears many times by the words she wrote about me. It was bad enough living with her daily anger, her frequent loathing of my mere existence, and her constant reminders of my failings. Yet reading it on paper, long after the event took place, was more distressing than I ever imagined it could be. And it was often just as painful to read my own.

Through the grief and frustration I often felt while doing this project, I was reminded once again how much letting go hurts and yet, to get to the other side of it, you have to fully feel the pain. And through that process, I finally let go of this only child of mine. I can now speak to her as the adult woman she is. I still want to jump in and fix things and sometimes struggle to keep my mouth shut. I realize she has her own life to figure out, that I do not have all the answers and cannot control her process. And journaling together was an important part of the journey that got us to where we are today.

MAGGIE

Letting go sucks. Let's face it. You can try to justify or sugar-coat it—say that it's an unavoidable part of life, and it's better and healthier to accept it—but it still sucks. Humans by nature do not like change and that's just what letting go involves. It means change and losing something. And what comes next might even be better than what you originally had, but there's no way to know that. All there is in that moment is loss. So yeah, it sucks.

Like a lot of kids today, I have divorced parents. They split up when I was five, which gave me just enough time to remember what life was like with my parents together, but not enough time to see why they didn't work. All in all, a really crappy way to be. And it kind of defined Mom's and my life for a long time. Which was both a good thing and a bad thing. It meant she put all of her energy and focus on me. She never missed a game, or a concert, or a play. Pretty much everywhere she went I went. And vice versa. She started substitute teaching at my school so she'd get home the same time I did, so I wouldn't have to be a latch-key kid. But like I said, she put all her focus on me. Which, by the time I was in high school, was a very bad thing. I couldn't escape from her. I was ready to be treated like an adult, and she couldn't let go of the little girl playing dress-up with her high heels. And I guess it's either a credit to our relationship that I didn't do the whole crazy rebellion thing, or I'm just a super boring person. I hope it's not the latter.

I have to admit, when Mom first thought up the idea of a journaling project, I didn't really put a whole lot of stock in it. I figured it could be kinda interesting, but didn't really consider what sort of undertaking it would be. When we first started the actual writing, I tried to think of it just as a normal journal, where I could vent all my frustration about my mom and my life. Unfortunately, I've never been good at keeping up a journal. I have about ten I've started over my life and never finished. So making it through this project was a bit of a struggle. My excitement was probably at its peak when I picked out our journals. I was more interested in finding something pretty than thinking about what I would use it for. I guess I like the idea of a journal more than the journaling itself. Although to my credit, I did fill my *Water Lilies* journal a lot more than my *Keroppi* journal in elementary school.

One thing Mom thought would be important was to pick some specific events for us to write about, in order to provide the dual perspective. Sometimes it was a significant moment, like my sweet sixteen party (such an awesome night) and the 2000 election that we followed closely. Other times, Mom would decide that we should both write about a fight we had, in order to truly get the complete picture. But usually we wrote whenever either of us remembered to pick up a pen. There were lots of times that we were so busy that having to write in the journal became a chore. I know Mom wanted to give up sometimes, and there were probably lots more times I wanted to abandon ship. Usually, when we were exhausted or totally pissed at each other, the thought of writing seemed like complete torture. So, I didn't write. And neither did she.

Mom had promised me that this wouldn't control our lives. Even when it seemed like that was exactly what was happening. I have to admit, through all the fighting we did over it, we became closer, and I think most importantly, we learned how to communicate with each other. Something that has served us well in our relationship today.

Mooring Comes Undone

Bending over to sprinkle cleanser
in the bidet   I am once again   bathing
my daughter   little red tug boat   floats
around chubby legs   her open face
churning with delight   as tubby toes
tilt and toss   the plastic vessel.
Pudgy fingers slap liquid surface
grasping at bubbles   as tug leans
and bobs   its grinning captain
twirling about.

An inconsolable hand scrubs
as tears slosh into basin   that
bathed baby girl years ago
who will soon drift off   to
distant ports   and yes   my
mooring   has already
come   undone.

chapter one

She Loves Me ... Not

CAROL   Monday, April 3, 2000, 10:55pm

On Saturday, while trying to get online to catch up on email and research publishers, a message appeared saying that I couldn't. One of Maggie's screen names was in use. How could this be? She's at her dad's and it's not after 11pm. We had an agreement. She reneged. Do all 15-year-olds do this? Did I? Who am I kidding?

So I called tech support. A guy named Thermon answered. "My daughter swindled the Master Screen name," I said. I had my doubts he'd be of any help.

"We can fix that," he said.

Oh, Thermon. His intoxicating words got me high. And in a moment's time, I possessed the new password for the master screen name. I was the Captain of our cyberspace. There was one major catch. Maggie would be pissed and I'd have to deal with it.

She called me yesterday. "Mom, what the heck's going on? I can't check my email." That's when I spilled the beans.

"I've got the master screen name now."

She slammed the phone in my ear. I rummaged through the cabinets, searching for chocolate. I found a stash I'd hidden in the Van Gogh mug. Not nearly enough to appease my anxious heart. I waited a while before I called again, and prayed Teresa, the new wife, wouldn't pick up. I left a message for Maggie and

Rickey. "Would you call me? Please?" They did, hours later, when I was out for my walk.

Listening to the message, I knew it was a good thing Maggie found out about this at her dad's. He seems better with her than I am these days. I paced. Stuffed fistfuls of corn chips in my mouth. And tried to write as I waited for her to get home. Rickey came in to buffer the blow.

She screamed. "What the hell you think you're doing? You're invading my privacy. How could you betray me like this...?" I trembled from her words. Tried to get her to see my point of view and failed miserably.

"I will not check your email," I said.

"Yeah, right, Mom." She stormed out of the kitchen and fled to her room.

MAGGIE   Monday, April 3

I have decided, when the cards are down, my mother is a manipulative bitch. I love her. I have to. She gave birth to me. But sometimes I *really* hate her.

So now, she has my password and can read my emails if she wants. It is a complete invasion of privacy. Like having the key to someone else's journal. Today she put Dad in the middle of this. When he brought me home, she began using him as a 'shield,' and refused to tell me what my password was. Dad tried to get her to tell me, but she refused. She also fucked around with the time limits (which she has now fixed). But she just threatened to change them because I stayed online for an extra half hour.

That's what she does all the time. She threatens. But it's usually threatening to cancel the Internet. O.K. what's her total: 1) manipulating; 2) privacy invader; 3) blackmailing; 4) liar. Oh yeah, she's a great mother. One I can really trust. Then she goes and blames this all on me, saying I purposely got the master account. The only reason I did was because I put my screen name in first. She was taking too much damn time thinking up a name (which by the way is a sucky name). I mean, using your initials? So lame. Seriously, she is totally trying to pin this on me. Even Dad thinks she's wrong.

CAROL   Tuesday, April 4, 2000, 11:15pm

Cripes! I need to stop and ask myself who's in charge here? Me or the friggin' guilt? And take some deep breaths. Ma used to count to ten. Her spiritual practice for mothering.

I'm having trouble letting go. I'm so confused about what to do most of the time. I need to be in control. Shit. We both do.

MAGGIE Monday, April 5

God, if she knocks on my door one more time, I swear I'm gonna strangle her. *Go a-way!* Does she not understand English?! Seriously. One more knock.... I've had it.

CAROL Wednesday, April 5

I'm thinking of the day I brought Maggie into the world. I felt so sick from the epidural and c-section, I could hardly hold her. I asked them to take her away. This is payback for that. I know it is.

MAGGIE April 7

It's been one of those "curl up in a ball and die" days.

CAROL April 8, 10:35pm

What happened to my little girl? The one who used to idealize me. Who followed me around wherever I went. Who sat on my lap and thought I was the smartest person on the planet. I was the center of her world, her universe, and now, I'm just this thing she has to put up with. How long will this go on? I hate to even imagine what she's writing about in her journal!!

MAGGIE April 8

TOP TEN (OTHER) REASONS I HATE HER:
10. Bag Ladies have more fashion sense than she does;
9. She's destroyed any chance of me fulfilling my
    life-long dream of being an addict;
8. Laughing at yourself does not constitute a funny joke;
7. Her driving's so bad that NYC cabbies would refuse
    to drive with her;

6. Cows chew more quietly than she does;

5. Her crying could replenish the Quabbin;

4. Her secret plot to destroy my social life
   may soon lead me to matricide;

3. She hovers like the Good Year blimp;

2. She breathes like a stalker on the phone;

1. But the number one reason to hate Mom
   is her outright existence!!

CAROL April 10

Remember when she used to take hikes with you in the woods? Pick apples and blueberries and strawberries with you? Ride bikes, cruise to the library, and roller skate with you? Remember when she held your hand? Gave you spontaneous hugs? Told you that she loved you, without you saying it first? Remember the days she couldn't wait for you to get out of bed so she could just be with you? Sigh.

MAGGIE April 10

Buffy's on tomorrow! How sad is it that that's the only reason I want to go down to Dad's? I wish I felt more welcome there.

CAROL Thursday, April 13, 12:17am

Maggie came home from Rickey's tired, stuffy, and irritable. I was anxious about how she'd greet me. What can I say? She is the soul of my day, my steamy cup of tea, my hot bath. My body was tense all day, harboring a low-grade headache. The junk food didn't help. We're still traipsing on slim ice.

I keep making the same mistakes with this Internet stuff. One of the things I despise about single parenting. The number of mistakes needed to learn a particular lesson is disproportionate to the value of the lesson being learned. Surely one of Einstein's theories.

God, I hate this.

We watched *Guiding Light*. Glad she still does that with me. After, we fought over online time, until I gave in. I'm afraid she won't like me. I wanted her to clean house with me. I'm freaking out about next weekend. I need her help. She wasn't feeling well. I didn't care. I made a big stink about how she never helps me and got into a big fight. I bolted for the kitchen, looking for chocolate. To push down the guilt. I need to apologize for dumping on her. Shit. My life is an endless string of apologies.

I don't remember Ma ever apologizing. Her motto being "Love is never having to say you're sorry." And what my adolescent brain got from that was I needed to be perfect—like her. Who never seemed to make mistakes. The truth was, she couldn't see her mistakes or wouldn't admit them.

I'm stressed. My whole friggin' family's coming to celebrate Johnny's birthday. From New York, New Jersey, Maryland and Vermont. Is my brother really turning 50? I am *so* freaking out. I hate playing hostess. As Eeyore would say, *Pathetic!*

MAGGIE April 13

Things are better between Mom and me. I'm sick, so she made me tomato soup. But I still feel crappy. Mom and I haven't worked everything out with the Internet, but I've let it drop for now. Once things have settled back down, then we can discuss it.

CAROL Friday, April 14

I dropped Maggie at her dad's today. It's such a relief to have the house to myself. Then why is my heart breaking in two? How could I possibly be missing her?

MAGGIE April 19

Dingle "accidentally" dropped his goggles out the window today so he could escape biology. Ms. Roberts let him go out to get them. Yeah, he never came back.

CAROL Thursday, April 20, 11:55pm

I've created a princess. She'll need a maid when she leaves here. Not getting her to help more around the house is *REALLY* bugging me. I need to take a course in this.

I look at her now—she's got Rickey's blue eyes—and those thick Irish lashes are his too. Thank God she got my nose. I hate this. I'm still obsessing about the past.

She was only five when he left. Four months after I started recovery. I was so scared. I hid in my room a lot. To release the steam that was shooting out my ears from all the rage. I remember hiding just to get away from her. Poor thing. I was afraid I would scream at her. Or hit her. Or take a drink. Back then she was so small and sweet. She's now 5'7" and is a force to be reckoned with.

Of course, I thought it was my job to make up for Rickey leaving. I didn't want to put the burden on Maggie. I took it way too far by taking on everything that needed to be done around this house, which hurt her in the long run. What we have now is a severe case of domestic deprivation. There's still time to whip her into shape. Fat chance. Where's Martha Stewart when I need her?

My real problem is I want her to like me. She's always mad at me. I don't want to feed her any more ammunition. God, it's painful to parent like this.

MAGGIE April 20

Go away, Mom! I swear I can feel her lurking outside my door. The anal-retentive freak who has gone cleaning crazy. Who cares what the house looks like?

CAROL Monday, April 24, 9:40pm

I'm already in bed—still bushed after our weekend with family. I made a yummy meal on Saturday for Sui, Phil, and Ma. Eat your heart out, Martha baby! Baked salmon with fresh asparagus and wild rice; apple pie heaped with Ben & Jerry's French vanilla ice cream. Yum. Company's good for us. Besides eating well, it keeps us from fighting.

On Sunday, we met at Paisano's, fourteen of us decked out in silly hats, all set to lavish my brother with goofy gifts, wise cracks, raunchy jokes, and hours of screeching laughter. When the management had enough, we schlepped the crew back to our house for story-telling and more food. Sui, Phil, Ma, Johnny, Kathy, Jill, Lauren, and Joe.

Maggie sat close to me, delighting in the stories I told of my teen years. Like the night I dressed as Maria, borrowing a nun's costume from *The Sound of*

Music wardrobe, our high school play that year. I drove to Grunnings with friends, sauntered into that local hangout and bought a pack of cigarettes. Then stopped home, rang the door bell and almost gave Ma a heart attack (she thought a nun from school had come to say I was dead) .

She loved the story about the night I almost got shot during one of our pool hopping sprees. That night, we jumped into Ronnie Quarnaccio's convertible. And as he squealed away, we swore we heard gun shots ringing through a blistering summer breeze.

We wound up on the trampoline. Sui's first time. Johnny, Mag, Sui, and I bounced together. After three jumps, Sui laughed so hard, she peed her pants. The harder we laughed, the more she peed. My sister's bladder problem is an old family joke. We're certain she flunked potty training.

After they left, Maggie and I wrangled over computer time. Fighting about control. My not giving her enough. These struggles are killing me. I need to let go. But I don't know how.

I'm losing my baby, my only child, and I want to hold on for dear life. We went to bed mad. We said we'd never to do that again.

I woke at 2:00—still feeling agitated. I was about to switch off my light, when she knocked on my door. It was 3:30. "Mom, I can't sleep." Her voice sounded so young. We tottered back to her room. I stayed past 5:00. It was sweet—laying beside her, massaging her back, soothing her to sleep. My heart is melting.

MAGGIE April 24

We all went out to Paisano's, which would have been fine if it weren't for two things: my family is psycho and a friend from school works there. And there we were, the whole lot of us, sitting in Paisano's with stupid hats on, and Janet, of all people, comes over to wait on our table. Ack! I was praying for the floor to swallow me up. And of course, it didn't. It was Ma who talked me out of my funk, and I finally got into the festivities. I tried fried calamari for the first time. It was surprisingly good. And I got to hang out with my cousins, who I hardly see. I wonder if everyone's family is this crazy.

CAROL   Tuesday, April 25, 8:40pm

I heard from Greg Joly, my editor at Bull Thistle Press. He doesn't even own a computer. His letters are missives from another time. He likes the title I chose for my poetry chapbook. "DIVORCE PAPERS." The memory still haunts me.

> *I kick leaves*
> *already curled*
> *at the edges*
> > *searching*
> *for fragments*
> *of my heart.*

> > *My chest   torn open*
> *as*
> > *the deputy sheriff*
> *handed me*
> > *divorce*
> > > *papers…*

Does anyone really get over these things?

MAGGIE   April 25

I hate my eyebrows. I'd like to shave them off and draw in my own. But Mom keeps telling me to leave them alone. That someday, I'll be glad to have them. To me, they look like one big eyebrow growing across my forehead. Uni-brow. She thinks they look like Brook Shields' brows.

CAROL   Wednesday, April 26

I used to love to cook. My initial creative expression long before I ever wrote a single word, cooking was my chosen profession for ten years.~~I was a self-taught graduate of the culinary arts, accululating credits from hours of loitering in my moher's kitchen, a woman~~ My mother, whose sense for the perfect ingredient was rivaled only by the likes of Julia Child and James Beard, acted as my professor in the culinary arts, and I accumulated credits as I loitered in her kitchen. ~~My mother was a natural born cook. I got the knack from her.~~ *But when I reconnected with an old lover—my very first lover, in fact, and the first man* ~~I've~~ *I have known intimately since my marriage ended—everything my mother had passed on to me fluttered out the kitchen window.*

Maybe I'll send this to *Salon*. Gulp. Could be perfect for "Mother's Who Think" (in my case, Mother's Who Strain Their Brains to Think). Maybe with some recipes.

Nah. Just keep writing.

MAGGIE   April 26

Echo

You stand there with a smile pasted on your face, screaming inside.
And you wonder why nobody looks up. Nobody cares.
You are just this person standing there with a smile on your face.
The Masses stream past, walking the walk and talking the talk.
You can't walk the walk, you trip and fall.
You can't talk the talk, you don't know the language.
You are just this person standing there with a smile on your face.
A dummy with your face asks why are you here.
A trick of a bad magician. Pick a card, any card.
Someone is screaming. It is you.
Everyone disappears.
And you are just this person standing there. A smile on your face.

CAROL   Thursday, April 27, 9:25pm

Got another lousy night's sleep. I'm too excited about seeing Len this weekend.

Seeking sleep   as visions
of your ~~upcoming~~ *visit*
swirl through my tempes~~tuous~~
tuous torso   a cyclone of
desire that won't be
tamed   ~~it's~~ like searching

for a viridian secret   in
a sea of midsummer
moss   each quickening
breath   drawn in ~~as~~ a
~~gentle~~ reminder
of the stormy
night you
produce
in me.

Hmmm. I guess it could work. No, I need to keep *upcoming*. Anyway, fatigue is good sometimes. It taps me on the shoulder and nudges me to let go. Helps me to surrender when that's what I need to do. Most of the time, I need a sledge hammer.

I trudged through this day, then fought with Maggie when she got home. We're still sparring over Internet access. Mag knows swearing at me is not allowed. So yesterday was a no access day. She tested the limits and badgered me most of the night. I held my boundary. Yea me!

I have my period. I'm tired and cranky. How we squeezed out a good evening is beyond me. We ended the day with a movie—*To Kill a Mockingbird*—one of our favorites. We're film fanatics.

I feel strong right now. A more solid and reliable Mom. I may live to regret these words. Does a snake drag its genitals?

MAGGIE April 27

Things were okay today. It was day one of my period and I had major cramping and fatigue, so that didn't help. I had been PMSing all week and I know I was being a bitch. But so was Mom. She's gotten into this total control-freak mode over the Internet, which was just what I didn't want to happen. That was the whole point of me having the master screen name, so she couldn't mess with the controls. I should add that to my list. Control-freak.

MAGGIE April 29

I just finished watching *When a Man Loves a Woman* and I can't stop crying. It's been at least a half hour, but I can't stop. I should know better than to watch that movie. It always hurts so much. For so many reasons. Because Meg Ryan and Andy Garcia make it work, I mean, their marriage doesn't end. Because Meg Ryan plays an alcoholic and it feels so real. Her bottom may have been a lot lower than Mom's, but the feelings are just the same. The movie just makes me think about what our lives were like for so long. And I realized, I have never talked to my friends about it. I never told my friend, Ann, what it was like to be on our own. That we both used to cry everyday. That I remember waiting on line for food stamps. That the reason I got pneumonia was because we couldn't afford to turn up the heat. That until I was in 7th grade, all I wore were hand-me-downs and clothes from a thrift shop. And it hurts so much. That our lives were like that. And that Dad was either oblivious or incapable of helping. That he seemed so unaware that Mom wasn't in any state to have to heal herself and raise a child all on her own. It just wasn't fair Mom had to do that.

But because she did, I am forever grateful. No matter how hard our life was, it could have been so much harder. But it still hurts. And I wonder if I will ever stop hurting. I'm not sure how to do it. And most of the time, it doesn't even bother me. I really shouldn't watch that movie, but I can't seem to stop myself whenever it's on. So I just have to do something to make myself feel better, because I'm on my own with this writing. It's helped, so that's good. I guess I should go to sleep now. It's 3:00. At least I've stopped crying.

CAROL Monday May 1, 8:30am

Sui and Phil stopped by to pick up the jacket Ma left last weekend and gave me a break from my writing. Wrote six poems about my time with Len. Poured out of me like honey from a jar.

Walking to your car   seizing kisses
from lips I already miss   we hedge
around farewells   our weekend tryst
nearing its end…

Before I left to pick up Maggie, Sui ran out to their car. She brought in a small square package wrapped in brown shopping-bag paper. Dad's ashes had finally shown up after 15 years.

We thought they were lost for good. Phil needed my dad's death certificate for something, called the funeral home, and found out they were there. Good grief. We ended our short visit arguing about what to do with them, my brother-in-law and I wrestling over my dad's remains.

Maggie's bus was late. I sat in the car, breathing deeply to halt the pain—till she slipped in the seat beside me—a solace to my heart. A slew of news rattled from her lips and I was glad to have her familiar voice ringing in my ears.

We spent the evening in parallel play—she on the computer—me watching a tape of *Guiding Light*. She joined me near the end, anchoring me to a safe harbor.

MAGGIE May 1

Len was here over the weekend while I was at Dad's. It totally freaks me out thinking that he was here. I mean, he's really nice and all, but he's invading my territory or home base, whatever. Not to mention that I don't want to know what happened. BAD mental picture. It's bad enough thinking about your parents like that, but someone who isn't my dad, it's just really hard.

MAGGIE May 2

Can she not read? MOM, STAY OUT! And the woman calls herself a writer.

CAROL Tuesday May 2

Dad's ashes are turning me inside out. After all this time, I'm finally getting the closure I need. I take them to bed with me and cradle them in my arms, dreaming of Dad.

During the day, I tote the box from room to room, transporting his love as I amble through the house. I miss you, Dad.

MAGGIE May 3

I've been in a mopey mood all day. I have no idea why. Maybe it's the weather. Too much gray. But I felt crappy all through school, and coming home didn't help at all. Thus, tonight called for a viewing of *Titanic*. Nothing like a heart-jerking romance to make you feel better about your own life. I've seen the movie so many times. I still have my ticket from when Ann and I saw it for the first time in 1997. We waited in line for almost an hour and got the last two seats. We got stuck way up front, and to the left, and sobbed through the whole thing. Ah, good times. So that memory in and of itself is making me feel better. Yay!

CAROL Thursday, May 4, 11:03pm

I feel blessed. Gratitude has governed the day. My 3:00 massage helped. Marcia's strong, gentle hands knead away tension that's always there. The smell of lavender intoxicates me. I slip right into that zone of relaxation. If only I could bottle it up and sip on it now and again. Whoa. Been there, done that.

I also had a great writing week—7 poems, and this essay for Salon is coming along.

My lover, a luscious French-Italian melange of a man, apprenticed at Le Cordon Bleu in London. He was a private chef for years, preparing meals for the rich and famous, waltzing around the kitchen like Fred Astaire, his hands in sync with his taste buds, his feet in rhythm with the cadence of the KitchenAid.

I ~~first~~ fell in love with him when I was 18, a naive college freshman, with only a few good recipes to my name. Three years my senior, he introduced me to french fries with vinegar, scrambled eggs with Tabasco, ~~and lovingly rendered my first banquet of libidinous pleasures~~ and sex. After five years of on-again, off-again romance, we went our separate ways.

Two years ago—with three broken marriages, three children, and three decades between us—we were reunited ~~two years ago~~ at a family gathering. We spent the weekend catching up and flirting, bantering over ~~which brownies were best one of us~~ who made the better brownies. Mine ~~which I had brought to the party,~~ caused everyone to drool over their rich chocolatey moistness, which surely made his gastronomic blood boil.

Len is my muse. He's my cousin's cousin and a family friend for years. It must be our history. I can't believe I'm actually dating my first lover again. Could it really be 30 years ago?

Last weekend, we lit a bunch of candles, turned out the lights, and danced in the same spot for an entire album. We used to call it vertical sex. Why does he have to live so far away?

I'm still on fire.

Even wrote some song lyrics.

You turn me inside out with that deep gaze of yours,
Those eyes that know me better than I do,
You always leave me breathless, with just one look,
Don't stand a chance when I'm alone with you.

MAGGIE May 4

Mom just got grandpa's ashes the other day. He's been dead for almost 15 years. They've been at the funeral home this entire time. It's made me think about Dad's and Mom's death, which I know will happen someday. It scares me a lot to think of that.

CAROL Friday, May 5, 11:40pm

I worked on one of my YA novels. *Hillary Garfunkle's the Name.* I love the first paragraph.

Mom says I came into the world reluctantly. When the doctor tried to pull me from her belly, I grabbed a rib and wouldn't let go. Jeez, can you blame me? Here I was, perfectly content. Surrounded by this posh womb. All of a sudden, they want me to make my debut as a human being, spotlights and all...

It could be Maggie telling her own birth story. I think I'm ready to submit it somewhere.

I've never felt more creative and full of who I am. The effect ripples through my relationship with Mag. I'm happy when my writing flows well. And I take it out on her. I'll be glad when I can start earning some money as a writer. For now, my unemployment and the child support Rickey gives me will have to do.

MAGGIE May 5

I just found out that Mrs. Warren was a trucker before she became an English teacher. She used to drive tractor-trailers all over the country. I can just see her sitting up in the cab of her Mack truck, radio blasting some country music station, cruising along some badass highway on the way to California or somewhere out west. And maybe taking a break to do some quilting. She loves that stuff. Odd combination. But it works for her.

CAROL Saturday, May 6

We moved Maggie's computer from the family room to her second bedroom. The one she uses when the weather's warm. This big old house affords such a luxury. I knew no matter what she did as we moved the stuff, I needed to keep my mouth shut. Joanie tells me to pick my battles. I'm trying to treat Maggie with more respect now. She's no longer a child. Her constant reminders are helpful. Yeah, right.

We pushed and tugged the boxes loaded with components up the stairs, then heaved them down the hall. We didn't have one fight! A victory in itself. We laughed most of the way. Keeping my mouth shut actually works. I wonder if Einstein knew about this!

After situating things, we watched the *Guiding Light* tape from yesterday. Something we can do together without getting mad. I need to find new ways to be with her. Even if it feels uncomfortable. Listening to her music often does. But she likes when I know the words. Sometimes she even lets me sing along. For years, she'd scream when I did that. This kid has trained me well.

We ate tuna and chopped pickle sandwiches for dinner and howled over an episode of *Seinfeld*. Afterwards, Maggie read poetry to me, one by her classmate, Sam Wallace, *…and she danced with him until she wanted to take the heeled shoes off and drink punch…* from the creative writing chapbook Mr. Mercus puts out each year.

We had a moment on my bed, talking about my father's ashes, when Maggie encouraged me to let go of old resentments I still have about Ma, so I don't have any regrets. Tears bathed her eyes when she spoke the words, "Mom, you don't want to feel bad about yourself when Ma dies," wondering if she was really thinking about herself and me. This was one of those nights I slurp up like a kitty, whose purr can be heard on the other side of town. The house was swimming in love, our hearts as wide as the sea.

MAGGIE May 6

Ann and I worked at the blood drive and car wash that was hosted by her church. This was the second year in a row that we did. I just wish I was old enough to give blood. But I'm also glad I can't. I hate needles. The car wash was lots of fun. It was wicked hot out, so getting soaked was a good thing. Even if Ann's little sister made us listen to crappy teeny-bopper music. Britney Spears, ugh.

CAROL Sunday, May 7

It's so freakin' hard for me to keep my mouth shut. Just ask my mother. She used to say my worries poured off my tongue like Niagara Falls.

I try to detach—to not get hooked by the drama between Maggie and me—to act, rather than react. I'm slowly learning to keep my lips zipped. I think I can, I think I can….

But it's one of those freaking-out-about-money days. I have lots of those. It's almost impossible for me to detach when I'm like this.

MAGGIE May 7

Someone recently asked me why I want to be a marine biologist. And I felt like such a dummy. The only answer I had was, "I love the ocean."

Is that really reason enough?

I remember the exact moment I decided that marine biology was my calling. Mom and I were out on Long Island for a family reunion. I was 13 and we'd all gone to the beach. It was the first time I got to spend a significant period of time in the ocean. My cousins and I spent hours in the waves. We finally had to leave to catch our ferry, despite my begging that we stay longer. I just didn't want to get out of the water. And it was then and there that I decided I wanted to be a marine biologist. So I could always be by the sea. But don't I need more than that? Most people act out a love of the ocean by going on vacation at the beach. Am I crazy?

CAROL Monday, May 8, 9:50pm

I put my first seeds in the garden and hope they'll shoot up fast with this heat we're having. I love this time of year.

I finished two essays and got a call from Len. He phones me between clients. He whines about plunging stock prices. He likes his work as a stock broker, but frets all the time about the declining markets. I wish he'd go back to cooking.

He tells me stories about Luke and Anna and about his struggles as a single dad. He feels so guilty when he loses patience and yells at them. He knows I understand. And he talks incessantly about his brother, Ed. About their fights. About Ed's declining health. How his doctor says if he doesn't lose weight, he'll die. Everyone's mad at him for getting obese. Len worries about him all the time. I call them the 'odd couple.' Ed's the husband and Len's the wife. I wish they'd get divorced.

MAGGIE Wednesday, May 10

I am *so* obsessed with David Boreanaz. He's freakishly hot. And not the least bit married anymore. Yay for divorce. OK, yes, it's bad I'm happy he got divorced. But he's hot! Wicked hot! Anyway, Nat's in love with him too. So it's not just me. She's my only school friend who watches *Buffy*. We sit and drool over Angel. The 242-year-old vampire with a soul. That's not weird, is it?

CAROL Wednesday, May 10, 12:17pm

I went out to the car when Rickey dropped Maggie off. He teased me about my being in love. Said I had that look about me. It felt strange coming from my ex. It actually annoyed the hell out of me. It felt like being undressed.

chapter two

Egad! Mother's Day

CAROL Thursday, May 11, 10:55pm

Maggie came home from school exhausted and went right to her cave. To plug into her haven and check her Buffy fan club mail. I miss her when she doesn't watch GL with me. Her interest is waning, which is probably a good thing.

Thursday is our night to prepare our own separate meals. Mag used to cook for us on Thursdays, but we gave it up. Because I told her what to do. She didn't like that. It wasn't worth the fighting. So I made my salad, and Maggie snacked on junk food most of the night.

I've almost let go of the food stuff. I don't care what she eats. That's not entirely true. No, it's a lie. I'm just not telling her as much. A big accomplishment for me. She may disagree with this assessment. What am I saying? She disagrees with everything!

Tonight she asked me to come to her room. She wanted to share her *Buffy* clips. I interrupted too much. Asked too many questions. She lost her cool. I was just trying to act interested. Maggie's mix of exuberance and grumpiness confuses me. She wanted me there, but hated me being there. Shoot. Does this ever get easy?

MAGGIE May 11

It's so weird the things I recall from childhood. I actually remember all the songs from a stupid video I used to watch called Mother Goose Nursery Rhymes. It acted out all of the Mother Goose rhymes. Kinda bizarre. But it stuck w/me.

Mother Goose Stories
and Mother Goose rhymes;
Make magical memories,
and wonderful times.

If I can only do that on my history test tomorrow. Ack!

CAROL Mother's Day, May 14, 11:48pm

Not my favorite holiday. The day Rickey walked away from our family. He left at noon on Mother's Day. I watched the pick-up pull away. The tarnished brass bed in pieces, exposed, for all to see. Jostling in the flat of the truck as it escaped down the street.

Roaming the house, nails bitten beyond the quick, hugging my daughter more than she needed, I searched for remnants of the comforter we called our marriage. I gazed out our bedroom window, daffodils blurring in the spring breeze, and realized he must have taken that with him too.

CAROL Monday, May 15, 10:20pm

Today was a challenge. A backlash from Mother's Day. When Mag got home from school, I made a big stink about not getting a card from her. Shit. She's my only child. I hit her with it as soon as she walked in the door. Couldn't help it. Need more work on biting my tongue.

I took a much-needed walk. Ended up at the stream, by my favorite bed of moss. The tears poured down my cheeks. I cried for a long time. It still amazes me the stuff that crouches deep inside. When I got home, I apologized. So did she, 'cause while I was gone, she made me a beautiful card—a gesture that tenderized my heart.

MAGGIE May 15

Yesterday was Mother's Day. It was 10 years ago that Dad moved out. On Mother's Day. I still haven't forgiven him for that. Since then, M. D. has always been hard on Mom. She really gets into it and I don't. We got into a fight today about my planning on getting her flowers, but in the end, changed my mind.

The thing was, she called and said she was going to the movies. So I didn't get the flowers. Dad was the one who thought of it. Then Mom blamed me for pushing the idea out of his head. The way she said it, it sounded like she still loves him.

Get over him! It's been like 10 years and now he's married to the bitch-monster-of-death. Who despises Mom. And doesn't even know her. God, I hate Mother's Day. I've been bruised for life. There's 10 years of therapy.

CAROL Tuesday, May 16, 10:48pm

I make the same damn mistakes over and over till I finally get the lesson I need to learn. Cripes. I wonder if Einstein had to deal with this stuff. What about Martha baby…

MAGGIE May 17

Stopping to think for a minute can prevent so many problems. Teens have a much harder time seeing how their actions affect others. It would solve so many troubles and pain if narcissism could be amputated from our brains. Good luck with that.

CAROL Thursday, May 18, 10:48pm

I'm glad this week's almost over. I got three rejections for *Rose's Jump Shot*. My precious MG manuscript. I'm so sick of these freakin' things.

HarperCollins says, 'Thank you for submitting *Rose's Jump Shot* for our consideration. Several people in our office have had a chance to review it….' but, of course, they don't want to publish it.

Random House says, '…We've read the manuscript with interest, but we're sorry to report that we don't believe it would work well on our current publishing list'.

Great! How about next year? Or the year after that?

And 'Thanks for thinking of Dial, and best of luck in finding a home for your manuscript.' I have enough rejections to wallpaper my room. Using them for toilet paper might be a better idea. Grrrrr.

CAROL   Friday, May 19

I saw Renee today, my beloved therapist. I told her I wanted to shed the baggage that has shackled me much of my life, originating on the day my younger brother, John, was born. Arriving into the world an obvious troublemaker, his birth sent my mother straight to the sanatorium, the location consigned to tubercular patients back in those days. She stayed for a year and a half, as the alternative of caring for three kids under the age of six was not an option and I've been cursed with this reprehensible fear of abandonment ever since. "My days as a cloying, insecure, needy three-year-old girl are over," I resolutely exclaimed, having no idea what the process would entail.

MAGGIE   May 20

I don't know what was wrong w/ Mom today, but she was miserable. She had this horrible pain in her stomach. She said it almost felt like labor contractions. Ouch. So I just sat w/ her for an hour and read to her. I read her one of my favorite poems, from Elizabeth Barrett Browning's *Sonnets from the Portuguese*.

> *How do I love thee? Let me count the ways.*
> *I love thee to the depth and breadth and height*
> *My soul can reach, when feeling out of sight*
> *For the ends of Being and ideal Grace.*
> *I love thee to the level of every day's*
> *Most quiet need, by sun and candlelight.*
> *I love thee freely, as men strive for Right.*
> *I love thee purely, as they turn from Praise.*
> *I love thee with the passion put to use*
> *In my old griefs, and with my childhood's faith.*
> *I love thee with a love I seemed to lose*
> *With my lost saints, — I love thee with the breath,*
> *Smiles, tears, of all my life! — and, if God choose,*
> *I shall but love thee better after death.*

I don't know if it was the sonnet, or just me reading to her, but she seemed to feel better afterwards. Thank God. I can't handle seeing her in pain. If it feels this bad to me, I can't imagine how awful it is for her when I'm in pain. I once heard that having a child is like having your heart walk around separate from your body. I wonder if I could handle that!

CAROL   Sunday, May 21, 10:40pm

I have my father's ashes. Wrapped in a brown corrugated box, they sit in the middle of my kitchen table. A white label is strewn across the top, proclaiming in bold letters, **INSURED.** *I know that would please my father. He liked insurance. It made him feel safe...*

My first two essays were accepted for publication. Salon took the one I wrote about Len. They're paying me $300. The other runs locally in *Hampshire Gazette.* Pays $75. Look Ma. I'm freakin' rich!

I knew the next two weeks were intense for Mag, loaded with daily rehearsals for *The Crucible,* plus scads of schoolwork. So I offered to take over her dishwashing nights, in exchange for her doing them two extra weeks this summer. Am I losing my mind? She agreed right away. Then I remembered—she agrees to things and doesn't follow through.

I brought it up. She got defensive. "It's something I learned from you, Mom." The words were a hatchet, tearing my heart to shreds. I lashed out. It wasn't pretty. I took back my offer.

"Forget it. You can do the goddamn dishes yourself." She said it didn't matter. She wouldn't do them either way. I yelled some more. She escaped to her room.

I stewed for a while. Then tapped on her door. I knew I'd have to admit my failures. I sat on the edge of her bed, squirming with the truth. She did homework, watching *Stand By Me*, like I wasn't there.

I apologized to her for getting excited about things. For building up her hopes and not following through. "We were so poor," I said. "I was so depressed." A pantry full of reasons after her dad left. Tears stung my eyes. I knew Maggie had learned to distrust my words. And then—ta da—she apologized to me! She said she felt attacked and we both agreed to acknowledge that instead of lashing out. Gifts come in strange packages.

MAGGIE May 21

Today was Mom's unofficial Mother's Day. It didn't go well. This afternoon we got into this whole thing about how she can't trust me, and I said that she's been lying to me for years. It was a cheap shot, I know, but it was a defense tactic.

Later we went to see *The Virgin Suicides* at the Academy of Music. It was a well-made movie, but very depressing. Mom and I fought through the whole-thing. She always talks during movies, which annoys me immensely. I'd forgotten why I don't like going to the movies with her.

CAROL Monday, May 22

I need to practice what I preach. How can I expect my child to do what I'm not able to do? To follow through on a verbal commitment if I don't follow through myself.

Sometimes, I really hate being the adult.

MAGGIE May 22

I need to stop letting Mom get my hopes up. I'm going to try to avoid optimism and pessimism all together. Realists are hurt the least.

CAROL Tuesday, May 23

I went to my gyno today for the pain and what looked like a raw chicken liver that fell into the toilet on Saturday, as I curled over, clutching a pillow, on the seat. She gave me a D&C right there in her office, using this mini vacuum on my fibroids. I squeezed her assistant's hand so hard she gasped. Oh, the joys of *The Pause!*

MAGGIE May 25

Mom told me that Dad was married before he met her. To another Carol! I can't believe I've never heard about this. I can't believe that he's on his third marriage now. He's Ross Geller. *He is SO Ross!!* He got so mad when he found out Mom told me. He thought he should. I guess it makes up for him giving me the sex talk. I remember Mom was really upset; she wanted to be the one to tell me.

CAROL   Monday, May 29

Len came for the weekend. As usual, we spent most of our time in bed. We see each other once a month and honeymoon. Only thing missing is room service.

I still have the letters he wrote to me from Vietnam. Before I knew Rickey. We read them while we lollygagged in my bed. He was surprised by how insensitive he was back then. The pain of that time exploded in my chest. He held me and said how sorry he was. Told me stories about Vietnam. About the boy who taught him to play "Lady Jane" on the guitar, which he played before he left.

> *After you leave   I sit*
> *cross-legged on my ~~bed~~*
> *deserted bed   guitar*
> *straddling my aching lap*
> *fingers   caught up in strings*
> *pursuing chords to*
> *to Lady Jane   and*
> *I hear the ~~soft~~ voice*
> *of a Vietnamese boy*
> *softly singing*
> *Jagger's words*
> *as my tears plink*
> *the notes*
> *to the end*
> *of the*
> *song.*

MAGGIE May 29

I was just thinking about when I learned that Dad and Teresa were getting married, and how I actually found out about it from his friend, Harry. I couldn't believe Harry was sitting there, talking about wedding plans. I guess he thought I already knew. Well, I didn't. Dad felt guilty about it and took me out for dinner to Roy Rogers to apologize. I remember being SO mad at him and just sitting there, staring at the blinds on the window while he talked to me. I can't remember anything he told me, but I remember those blinds. A rose-colored tweed-ish material. Ugly. Just like that day.

CAROL Saturday, June 3, 11:00pm

Maggie took her first round of SATs this morning. Before delivering her to the test site, where hordes of anxious adolescents stood by padlocked doors waiting access to this barbaric rite of passage, we argued about food. She didn't want to eat. I told her she needed fuel for her brain. Of course, she won.

As she stepped from my car, she whisked off her jacket, exposing a pink tank top filled with her young ripening body, and flung the garment into the back seat. My heart stopped. First no breakfast and now no jacket. How will I ever get through this? I cried the whole way home. She's far too young for the rigors of this pre-college inquisition. I'm almost certain I weaned her from my left breast just the other day.

MAGGIE June 3

I'm way too young for SATs. Shit. I'm only a sophomore. What was my biology teacher thinking?! I don't want to even think about how I did. Anyway, college is so far away. I have no idea where I even want to go. I'll go anywhere but UMass. It really pisses Dad off when I tell him that. Although he gets more upset when I say I won't go to Westfield State. No way could I go to a school where he'd be all the time. Uh-uh.

CAROL Wednesday, June 7, 11:00pm

Maggie and I have been on a roller coaster the last three weeks. With my Salon debut, the photo-shoot for my *Gazette* piece, her over-scheduled week from hell, ending in SATs, I'm relieved that things are calming down. Some may disagree with this assessment if they'd been with us tonight.

Before fetching her at the late bus, a friend of hers called. She wanted Mag to call back right away. I relayed the message. When we got home, instead of calling, she hopped online. I was not in a great mood. I was still wrestling with the conversation I had with Len. He was so nasty to me. I just wanted to share my excitement about the newspaper coming to take my photo. "Is that why you called me?" he said. This was not the same man who was here with me 10 days ago.

> *…my rapture withers away*
> *only seconds after   I hang*
> *up   the phone.*

I wanted to call a friend. To talk it out. No. I wanted to throw her frigging computer out the window.

Tonight, during internet-free time [5:00-8:00], Maggie downloaded something online, jamming up the phone wires. I was pissed. This is my time to make calls. I lost my cool. Let's face it. I have very little cool at this stage of my life. It was a repeat performance of yesterday. I'm up to my eyeballs in *The Pause*. Some say nobody dies of menopause. My ass. Look at me cross-eyed and I cry. Which could lead to dehydration. You can die from dehydration. I know you can! *The Pause* has left its friggin' mark. Think I'll write an essay.

A single Mom for ten years, I'm am now a member of the menopause club, that sacred woman's ~~organization~~ society whose initiation requires the daily attendance ~~in~~ of classes in hormonal hell. Some of you may be tittering, but this is no laughing matter. Most of the time I ~~cry~~ bawl my eyes out, that is when I'm not straining what's left of my brain trying to remember what I muttered ten minutes ago to my ~~cruel~~ unrelenting teenage daughter, who seems to remember everything or makes it up as she goes along.

Sounds good. I'll use it. When I finally made my call, Maggie interrupted. She needed to call the friend—right away, mind you—which I'd nicely asked her to do when we first got home. I wanted to rip out her vocal cords.

MAGGIE June 7

Mom and I just finished watching a show about alcoholics and different treatments for alcoholism. Watching it made me so proud of Mom. Some people have developed a program in which they don't have to stop drinking completely, i.e., they still can't stop. Mom hasn't touched a drink in 10½ years. That's one hell of an accomplishment.

Mom and I also fought, surprise, surprise, about the Internet again. She was in the right for what she was upset about, but I'll be damned if I'll admit it to her.

MAGGIE June 8

Good thing I'm with Dad this weekend. If I have to spend one more second with her, I'm gonna scream.

CAROL Friday, June 9

I am so sick of getting up at 6:00. Waking her at quarter past. Hoping she'll be up by 6:30. Knowing it won't be 'til 6:40. Getting downstairs by 7:00—if she's lucky—to catch the freakin' bus by 7:10. It drives me crazy. Just two more years of this nonsense.

Only two more years of waking Maggie in the morning. Sigh.

MAGGIE June 9

I just started thinking about the time Mom and I were out at the Cape. After Dad and she split up. I was seven. Mom wanted us to have a real vacation, so she rented a little cottage in Wellfleet, down the street from where we used to go with Dad. Anyway, she went out to buy some groceries for us and came back with this bottle of fake wine. I *totally* freaked out. I made her pour it down the drain. She said it wasn't real and got mad at me. I ran into the woods behind the cabin and hid from her. And cried. I was afraid she was gonna start drinking again. I thought non-alcoholic beer and wine still had some alcohol in it. Enough to hook her again. Now I know better. But that day, I wanted to stay in the woods and die.

CAROL June 10

After seeing that show the other night, I've been thinking about how it was when I first stopped drinking. January 1, 1990. Rickey left in May. Frigging Mother's Day! Things were rough. I was scared out of my wits. Maggie crawled into bed with me every night. Now it sounds sweet. Back then it drove me crazy. Everything drove me crazy. My nerves were ragged, like my nails.

Obsessive thoughts wore me out. Shit. They still do.

How will I raise her by myself? How will I earn a living? How will I take care of this house? How will I pay the bills? How will I live without Rickey? How will I stay sober for the rest of my life?!! ACK! Shut-up, will you!…*and the longing's got me dangling methodically by my wretched feet…*

And the rage—it got so bad, I had to lock myself in my room. No wonder we have so many fights about control—Maggie must have been terrified in those early years.

I even took her to my AA meetings. That first year I went everyday. Sometimes twice a day. Three times on really bad days. Mag came with me on weekends and days off from school. Her presence kept me from drinking. And somewhat sane. Whatever that means…

MAGGIE June 11

This is really weird. I started thinking about the time Mom hid in the closet before Dad left. She was screaming at him and crying and I just remember her crumbling like a sack onto the floor of their bedroom closet. Dad kept telling her to stop, that it was bad for me to see this, but he didn't do anything to help Mom. I think this was right after she stopped drinking. Things were really bad back then. All she did was cry.

CAROL Wednesday, June 14, 11:56pm

Rough day. I had a blow-up with Len. Huge! He told me he couldn't see me for a while. This is when I miss the booze, just as the yearning has its rugged hands wrapped firmly around my miserable neck. And the desire—oh dear lord, the desire—it has a friggin' two-by-four shoved securely up my sorrowful crotch.

It's that damn job of his. He's a free spirit like me. He's not meant for the gluttony of the investment world. He's an artist. An actor, a musician, and a chef. That's what he should be doing. Shit. I was just getting used to our monthly dates.

My friends are unavailable. Or off on vacation. Sui's away for the month. At some campsite in northern Vermont. I need to talk to her. I rely on her sympathy. She's known Len for as long as I have. She listens as I go on about the things that bother me. I feel so abandoned and lonely. And so damn needy. Maybe that's why Len took space. Screw him, I say. God, just this once, could I ever use a friggin' drink. Sounds like I need a meeting!

MAGGIE   June 16

I just had another flashback, to the time I followed Mom down the street wearing her high heels. It must have been right after Dad left, when Mom took a run everyday. It helped her stay sober. I was playing dress up and started missing her so bad that I clopped down the street in her purple pumps. For 1/4 mile or so. I found her on her way back home. She was so surprised to see me, she started crying. And so did I.

CAROL   June 17

Aunt El and Uncle Chet called. Invited us to Wellfleet. It's just what I need. I wonder if Maggie will go with me. I hope so. The hell with Len!

CAROL   June 19

Maggie burst from Rickey's car in tears. Then ran into the house. He told her on the drive here how disappointed he was about Father's Day. Did he have to do this today?

I followed her inside. "Dad was so hurt I didn't get him anything for Father's Day," she said. Tears streamed down her cheeks.

"Oh sweetie," I said, and gave her a big hug. I held her and let her cry.

MAGGIE June 19

I hate Mother's Day *and* Father's Day. I think these holidays are incredibly stupid. I'm always the one who has to get them something. Major down side of being an only child.

chapter three

Matricide? Hmm, I Wonder

CAROL Friday, June 23, 11:56pm

On the way to the Cape, we stopped and had lunch by the Canal. We sat on the rocks, watching fishing boats cruise by. Seagulls screeched over our heads, as the smell of vacation oozed from salt air.

When we got to Wellfleet, a rush of memories streamed through the open windows. We had come here as a family—Maggie, Rickey and I—and seeing our old haunts made me teary.

It was good to be with Chet and El. They're a sturdy couple, 64 years of marriage to prove it. Mag and I stayed in the attic dorm; the big old room that stares out at the house we used to rent with Rickey, gazing over white cedar and scrub oaks onto Mayo Beach. Sharing this space is less comfortable now that she's older, but we managed. Just glad to be here.

I went to the Lighthouse for breakfast with Chet & El, and smuggled an order of blueberry pancakes and muffin back to sleepy Mag. That afternoon, we girls headed to the beach, leaving Uncle Chet to dabble with a painting at the cottage. We stopped at a fresh water pond. Mag and I frolicked in the water like sisters.

When we got back to the house, we rode bikes into town, gleaning items for dinner from Lema's—then dawdled at Mayo Beach, collecting shells, breathing the redolence of salt air, on our way back home.

After a succulent lobster dinner, we chuckled at my aunt and uncle's two-handed bridge game, both of them in their 80s, still as competitive as teens. We went to bed planning a jaunt on the Provincetown bike trail before heading back home.

The next day, Maggie was too tired, and my disappointment aroused my grief. I wept as I hurled clothes in my suitcase and loaded the car. I think I was crying about Dad, after receiving his remains. Their resemblance is so strong—Dad and Uncle Chet.

MAGGIE June 27

I got a fish. He's a red Betta named Oz. He's such a pretty little thing. I just hope I don't kill him like my goldfish.

MAGGIE June 29

I just finished *Wuthering Heights* for the second time. It is my *absolute* favorite book. It's completely heartbreaking. I don't know how anyone couldn't be moved when Heathcliff rants to the heavens, *"Catherine Earnshaw, may you not rest as long as I am living! You said I killed you—haunt me, then! The murdered do haunt their murderers, I believe. I know that ghosts have wandered on earth. Be with me always—take any form—drive me mad! Only do not leave me in this abyss, where I cannot find you! Oh, God! it is unutterable! I cannot live without my life! I cannot live without my soul!"*

CAROL Monday, July 3, 10:15pm

I got the list of the poems Greg is contemplating for the collection. I'm breathless. I am not dreaming this project. It's really going to happen. He's including "Holiday Weekend."

> *Pulling in the drive   I see his Jeep Cherokee   with its back to us.*
> *Fighting over   a knapsack   left   last week   at her dad's*
> *I ask her to bring it   to me   want to take it   home.*
> *Get it yourself   she ~~cries~~ spits   I threaten   with lame   consequences.*
> *I won't   go into   his house   too many ~~damn~~ high heels   laying about.*
> *How can I tell her that?*

She brings the backpack   heaves it into the car   turns to leave   then
looks back   sees me waiting   comes over   gives me a hug.
We do this a lot   fight back the sadness   that's wrestling

to be noticed.   I go to a movie   a box   of tissues   straddles
my knee   as I think of another holiday weekend
without her.

Maggie went to Misquamicut with Ann's family for the 4th. I went to Sui and Phil's. Sigh.

MAGGIE   July 6

Oh god. I *really* screwed up. I'm in big pain. The blisters are *so* bad. I'll never go out in the sun again. I finally understand the meaning of the song, "Wear Sunscreen." Shit. How will I *ever* make it as a marine biologist?

But bridge jumping was awesome! Robert, Lindsey and I had so much fun. Ann is *so* lucky to have such a hot brother. Most of the time she doesn't think so. Maybe she would if she joined in on the fun stuff. She refused to jump off the bridge. Bah. And never took Robert up on his offer to ride on his dirt bike. I did. It was wicked fun. But right now, I just want to die. Kill me now. Or at least cut my legs off.

CAROL   Thursday, July 6, 10:40pm

Had to pick Mag up in Rhode Island. She got a really bad sunburn. Her Irish skin can't tolerate much sun. Poor baby. Where the hell was her sunblock? Grrrr.

CAROL   Monday, July 10, 11:20pm

After three days of work on the "Cartales" project, I am deeply satisfied and relieved. Putting ten queries in the mail motivates me to tie up loose ends on that book proposal. And allows me to be available for Maggie's arrival home from day-one of the five-week babysitting job she's taken. Hope she can buy herself a car.

She actually came into the kitchen and rescued me from myself. I freaked out about making dinner. It's the damn *Pause*. I used to *love* to cook.

We watched *An American President*. I hope we can keep this good feeling between us the whole summer.

Later: Dream on Mama. I went to Maggie's room—and we fought over computer shutdown and bedtime. It got ugly. I stomped back to my room, licking the tears that were streaming down my face. She is pushing me to let go. I don't know how to do it!

MAGGIE July 10

She's a fucking bitch and I hope she rots in hell.

CAROL July 11

Hindsight is great, but comes at the wrong time. I keep telling myself, let go, let go, then let go some more.

MAGGIE July 12

Ann and I were so girly last night. I was over there hanging out and we played the name your children game. Emily even got in on it. Ann's little sister, who's not so little anymore. Makes me feel old.

But I've decided I want to name my children Olivia and Ethan. My backup names are Mia and Elijah. Or Joshua. Of course, I'm not even sure I want to get married. I mean, look how well it turned out for Dad. He's on his third. Maybe it's genetic. I've read that children of divorcees have less chance of succeeding in marriage than non-divorcees do. But I do want kids. And I don't want to do it alone like Mom. So I guess that means I'll get married. I just have to find someone who will make me want to marry him. Someday.

CAROL July 13

Maggie's birthday is coming up next month and she wants to have a co-ed sleepover. So we went to see Susan Gulick. I always hope she'll side with me. But she's officially Maggie's therapist, so she backs her, which pisses me off. I leave feeling slighted. Am I a bad mother or what? I made it perfectly clear at our session there'd be no people with penises sleeping over that night. None whatsoever!

Of course, I wouldn't bet the house on it. That girl can talk the hide off a hippo.

CAROL Friday, July 14, 10:50pm

I had another stormy conversation with Len. I pressed him about my coming to the family reunion Ed's having in a couple weeks. He kept hedging, then told me he wants to see other women. See other women? Go stick it in a meat grinder.

> *Thinking of our last*
> *conversation   the taste*
> *of your terror remains*
> *lodged between my teeth*
> *your plan to see other women*
> *stuck behind my upper left*
> *molar…*

Shit. I know he just wants some breathing room. Why can't he say—Carol, my sweetness, I just need a little space. Some 'no contact' time. Please don't take it personally. You know you are the love of my life. I swear—this is some archaic throw-back to high school. Grow the fuck up! I get so sucked up in this adolescent game. Other women? HA. Who wants to date a 56-year-old high schooler? Snap out of it, Carol. Get a life. Oh crap, this is my life.

I'm scared. Scared I'll lose him. And this passionate, healing relationship we have. It's not easy to come by at this age. Why have I trusted this man again with my heart? He's the love of my life. Loved him since I was a teen. Still think the meat grinder is a good idea.

MAGGIE July 15

Mom broke up with Len. He wanted to see other people and she couldn't be with him like that. Yea! I'm not happy she's sad, but glad he's gone. We were supposed to go to the movies to see *Me, Myself and Irene*, but we got there 15 minutes late. I didn't want to see it—having missed some—but Mom did. We got into a fight and finally left. I probably should've given in, but she was overreacting. Majorly.

We ended up shopping in Northampton. I got a kick outfit. When we got home, we watched *The Joy Luck Club*. Of course, Mom cried. I actually said I'd go back to the movies with her tomorrow. *Am I crazy or what?*

CAROL   Saturday, July 15, 11:14pm

Where are my friends when I need them? And my sister? Why isn't she home Mag agreed to schlep to the movies with me. We drove 45 mins to Cinemark. We got there ten minutes late. Maggie refused to go in. She's like I was at her age. Digs her heels into the friggin' ground and won't budge. Being the dutiful Mom, I gave in. Then tore out of the parking lot like someone on the verge of vehicular manslaughter. I was also starving, so we stopped for dinner.

Leaning across the table, I sucked it up and said I still loved her, even though she was an inflexible shithead. I believe in saying I'm sorry, but chose not to apologize. Some may even call this heel-digging.

After dinner, we went to Faces. Mag bought an awesome batik wrap-around skirt, with a stunning green top to match. She looked like a woman. I wanted to cry. I'm thinking about Ma. Wondering if I've totally forgiven her years of drinking (it's in the damn genes), for her lousy relationship with Dad, for her favoring Sui and my brother Phil, over Johnny and me. For her not being the mother I wanted her to be. I think she can die with my fully loving and accepting her. Next stop, sainthood!

MAGGIE   July 16

Would throwing Mom down the stairs be considered matricide? Hmm...I wonder.

CAROL   Sunday, July 16

When I was two and a half, Ma was hospitalized with tuberculosis. She stayed in a sanatorium for 18 months. I lived with three different families. First, I got dumped at Aunt Lu's. I missed my mom so much, I cried for three weeks. They couldn't handle me and shipped me off to Aunt Dot's. Still have vivid memories of getting burned by scalding water there. Someone finally brought me to Beazie's, where my sister was staying. It's hard to go back to that time.

When I was six, she got sick again. Hospitalized for another year. Tears fill my eyes as I write this. My fear of abandonment has followed me around like a relentless deer fly, leaving its mark on everyone I love. To lessen the fear, I would do anything to make a relationship work. Len once told me he felt my claws on his chest when we first dated in our twenties. After Rickey left, I fell into a similar pattern with Maggie, especially in her teen years. She calls it hovering. I wonder…did I do that with Rickey? I already dread her departure. It's a painful way to live.

MAGGIE July 17

If I ever do decide to get married, I think I want Pachelbel's Canon as my song. I just love it. It's both peaceful and exuberant at the same time.

CAROL July 17

I just found out Sue and Tony are moving to Illinois next month. How could she do this? Tell me her plans at the eleventh hour? She's been my dear friend for the last 10 years. What will I do without her? My world is crumbling around me—I cannot bear all this friggin' letting go.

MAGGIE July 18

I had the best dream ever last night. Prince William asked me to marry him. *sigh* God, he's gorgeous. And Mom had to go and ruin it by waking me up. Come back, Will!

CAROL Tuesday, July 18, 11:40pm

I woke with that gray veil of depression over my shoulders. I pampered myself with a few hours of reading in bed, then rallied to have a productive afternoon, doing revisions on "Yuck And Yum: A Veggie Tale,"and that blasted "Rose's Jump Shot." Why do I think being productive makes me a better person? Or takes away my sadness? I guess it beats wallowing in misery and self-pity. And if I make them good enough, some kind editor in the nether world of publishing might want them and pay me some real money.

When Maggie got home from Rickey's, we had one of the best evenings we've had all summer. The night ended in a fight over dishes. I fight to let go, then hold on for dear life.

MAGGIE July 19

Warped Tour tomorrow. YEA! And Mom and I had a good day today. The kids were sick, so I didn't have to baby-sit and I got to sleep in. Mom and I made tacos together and watched *Clueless*. I love that movie. The only fight we had was a few minutes ago.

I got kicked off AOL because of time limits while I was downloading something. Of course, it didn't finish the download, which pissed me off. I had to go down to do the dishes (there were way too many). I was still pissed off and took it out on Mom. I acted like a bitch and didn't finish the dishes. One point for the bitch. But which one? That's the question.

CAROL Wednesday, July 19, 12:10am

We made tacos tonight. Mag was in charge of grating cheese—chopping the carrots and lettuce—while I sautéed the garlic and meat. We worked side by side without a kernel of conflict.

A first for us. Munching our tacos, we watched *Clueless,* which Mag calls a modern-day *Emma* and is on her list of favorite films. I got a kick out of it—relishing this time with my daughter— finding more about how the teen mind ticks. How quickly we forget.

CAROL July 20, 11:53pm

Taking my daily walk as supper ~~hour~~
time closes in   my daughter is with
a friend at her first ~~rock~~ concert today
my inner chatter races along with
me   moving ~~itself~~ considerably faster
then my feet.   Quibbling with you
in my head   I grow ~~tired~~ weary of the
fight and ~~I~~ decide to run down hill
to the stream   passing over its
thin trickle with ~~all~~ the might of
a marathoner. Approaching the
pond   I forfeit the ~~fight~~ argument
as a blue heron rises from its
cool green waters   circling
the field where the small
lake sits   stopping ~~the~~ said
patter   dead   in its tracks
and I soar with the bird
this majestic creature ~~is~~
an oasis   in the midst
of   ~~all this~~ cerebral
chaos.

She got home in one piece. What would I do without poetry?

   What would I do without Maggie?

MAGGIE   July 20

Warped Tour rocked, even though I got sunburned. Again! Ann and I got stuck in a mosh pit and got pushed around, which made me panic till we escaped. We saw Save Ferris, which was a *wicked* good band. NoFX and Stone Temple Pilots played, and we left during Green Day's set, which sucked. Not the set, but having to leave. The whole reason we wanted to go was to see Green Day perform "Good Riddance." And we missed it, 'cause we had to meet Dad.

Actually, we were already late meeting Dad, and boy, was he pissed. I don't think I've ever seen him so mad. But hey, if he got me a cell phone, he'd never have to worry about where I am. I could've just called and told him we were gonna be late. But instead, we got lectured all through the tunnel into Boston, then there was silence on the Pike till we got back. It's wicked evil, that trick parents do to make their kids feel bad. Quiet condemnation is so much more effective than anger, and my dad certainly does it well. Evil!

CAROL   Monday, July 24, 12:10am

I've been moving in and out of anger and sadness for days now. Kicking things that get in the way, slamming doors, cabinets, with tears streaming down my face, anything to get rid of the pain I feel. I'm trying not to take it out on Maggie. "I'm so tired of being alone, I'm so tired of being alone…." My kingdom for a drink, she wistfully laments. Thankfully, depression hasn't taken hold. I was glad when Rickey dropped her off at 3:00—glad to see her again—glad for the distraction her presence provides.

I got stung by a mud wasp while mowing the lawn—suffered a mass of swelling around the sting—so Maggie's company felt comforting to me. After GL, I finished mowing. Then leveled some saplings and yanked out weeds that gobbled up my flower beds years before. A good place to get rid of the anger.

I came inside exhausted, thinking we'd go out for fast food, in place of the BBQ chicken I'd mentioned when Maggie got home. I don't like to bar-b-q much. Rickey used to do it. He loved standing in the backyard, drinking beer, flipping the burgers on the fieldstone fireplacewe built out of stones we collected ourselves. Even the Weber is too much work now.

This did not sit well with Maggie, and she wouldn't budge on the issue. I really wanted/needed her company. So, I wouldn't leave her alone. Asked her three more times to go with me.

It verged on begging. She kept saying, "NO!" I stomped down the hall. I heard her say, "You fucking bitch," as I retreated from her room. I landed in the bathroom in tears. I don't always get what I want, but usually get what I need. In this case, a good cry. Though I know it's not my daughter's job to take care of me, at times like these, I sure wish she would.

MAGGIE July 24

When I came home from Dad's today, Mom and I had a fight. She wanted me to go to Friendly's with her, but I didn't want to, 'cause I hate their food. So she went and I stayed home. Mom makes a much bigger deal about me staying home alone then I do, even for just a couple of hours. I actually like it.

CAROL Tuesday, July 25, 12:10am

Pennie and I leave for Germany next week. My first flight sober! Yikes!

MAGGIE July 26

Today had to be the most fun I've had all summer. Natasha called me and asked if I wanted to go to the DAR to make a movie. I haven't seen her since school got out, so of course, I said yes. Mom didn't like having to drive all the way up to Williamsburg, but oh well. So Nat's wicked cool dad, Peter, drove Nat, me, Jeanne, Chris, and Jack up to the DAR.

Turns out Chris wants to be a director. I guess he's made a few short movies with his beloved camcorder. He showed me the script, "A Perfect Day for Bananafish." A J.D. Salinger short story I read last year.

So we got to the DAR and Chris realized he didn't have any film. Very smooth. Jeanne had bound her chest for no reason. She was supposed to be Sybil Carpenter, who's a little girl, so she wrapped herself in an ace bandage. It took her forever to get it off. It sucks that we didn't get to film it. Jeanne and I got really into our characters. Sybil and Sharon Lipshutz (me) fight for the attention of Seymour Glass (Chris).

So we ended up just swimming in the lake. I didn't bring a bathing suit, so Nat let me borrow a T-shirt to swim in. Then we hiked around the lake, in bare feet. Lots of pain.

Even though we didn't get to make the movie, the whole day rocked. I hadn't really hung out with Jeanne since elementary school. And Chris and Jack are so much fun. I'm so glad Nat called me. We have to do that again, soon.

CAROL Thursday, July 27

I heard from Amy Hsu at Little, Brown. She likes my picture book, "The Day the Cows Got Loose." Mag and I used to walk down to the farm to pet the cows when she was little. We also watched them run haywire around the neighborhood that summer they got loose. In her letter Amy Hsu said, "We like Ida Mae's distinctive voice." Yahoo! I like her voice too.

Hit it, Ida Mae—

The day the cows got loose, Granny was taking her weekly soak in the tub,
while Grampy was knitting the last ~~two~~ rows on his purple scarf.
Ma was out back choppin' a load of wood,
while Pa was mending a hole in the roof of the chicken coop.
Sister was catchin' frogs down at the pond,
while brother was baking a loaf of his fa-vor-ite zucchini bread.
And good ol' Sally ~~well she~~ was buryin' a bone 'hind the shed.
The day the cows got loose, I was hanging upside down in the ol' apple tree,
dreamin' about how I'd ~~get~~ git famous some day.
Pa said since I watched them cows escape, I could round 'em up.
All twenty-six of 'em.

This manuscript has made its rounds. It's been to 13 editors before this. Sat with one for a year. Getting this letter makes me feel like Sally Fields. They like it, they really like it!!

Well, not that much. Amy also said, "however we feel the story needs a little more zing." Which means they kinda like it, but not enough to accept it as is. She said, "Do you have any ideas for an extra wrinkle to add to the plot? " Do I have any ideas? Three days before I leave for Germany? Egad. I just hope the blasted plane doesn't crash.

MAGGIE July 27

It turns out Jeanne and I both have crushes on cartoon guys. Prince Phillip from *Sleeping Beauty*, Trent from *Daria*, and Dimitri from *Anastasia*. And Natasha loves this guy Mamo-chan from *Sailor Moon*, which I guess is an anime show.

CAROL Sunday, July 30

I must have been out of my mind. Going to Long Island the weekend before we leave for Germany. But I wanted to see Len. To smooth things over a bit. Find out if he's really seeing other women. This love business sucks. I feel more like a teenager everyday. It's not earth shattering, just humiliating. And exhilarating at the same time.

I stayed at Kathy's and had fun with my girl cousins. Merry and I shared a room and howled. Like we did as kids. We're only six days apart. Have been friends forever. Hitch-hiking through Europe in our twenties was a high point in my life. She's also Len's cousin. She told me I needed to play it cool with him.

Under her watchful eye, I ignored him for half the party. When Merry wasn't looking, I flirted with him and with his brother Joe. I wanted to make Len jealous. See other women, will you! And smooth things over? I think not. Sounds more like what a 12-year-old might do.

Ed told me not to worry about Len seeing other women. He said that's what he says when he needs some space. Ha. Just what I thought! Grow up, will you!!

We strolled by the inlet before I left and got some time alone, which I wanted. We left on good terms. He kissed me and said he'd call soon. We'll see. We do that thing where one pursues, and the other runs away. I've been doing way too much pursuing lately. It's driven by fear. Could this possibly have anything to do with taking my first transatlantic flight without the aid of alcohol, plus leaving Maggie home? A knot tightens my stomach just thinking about it.

MAGGIE Aug 1

I love trains. They're much more fun to ride in than cars. Ann and I played chess and checkers on her little travel game set, and we chowed down in the dining car. For the first time, I put cream cheese on a bagel and liked it.

I also love sleeping in Aunt Susie & Uncle Phil's RV. We stayed up wicked late last night, listening to music and playing cards. Ann taught me how to play 'spit.' I suck at it, but it's fun. We got kind of violent about it, though. Ended up slapping each other's hands more than the cards.

Today Aunt Susie took us to see *The Patriot*. What a sad movie. But it was worth the tears to see Mel Gibson and Heath Ledger on-screen together. Yummy!

CAROL   Wednesday, August 2

I love Munich. Pennie and I are having such a blast. As always. And they haven't kicked us out of Germany yet!

This is our first long trip together. I worried about how we'd get along, being together 24/7. We've been friends for years. Met her when we worked in the kitchen at Beardsley's. But as a writer, I'm used to being alone. Anyway, seems to be working just fine.

Our hotel sits facing the *Englischer Garten*, a retreat spanning 3½ miles, twice the size of Central Park. We can sun bath topless if we want. The Isar River, which borders the garden, has a series of canals that weave verdant waters through the city. The jade-green color amazes me each time we cross over one of these inland waterways.

The food is incredible. Every morning we feast on a huge buffet. We start out with platters of fresh fruit, followed by bowls of muesli and crème, decked with fresh raspberries, then finish our meal with freshly made waffles or omelets to order. Along with infinite breakfast wursts. My favorite is weisswurst. But, of course, mien Herr!

MAGGIE   August 3

Today was fun, even though I felt wicked crappy. I've had a sore throat all day, and it just keeps getting worse. Ugh. But it was worth the pain to go to the Ben and Jerry's Ice Cream factory. We got to see how the most delicious ice cream in the world is made and ate free samples. I am now in love w/ Cherry Garcia.

After going to the factory, we visited the Von Trapp Family lodge. It was this huge estate that's been turned into a museum. We saw Maria's grave. Apparently she wasn't the joyful nanny that Julie Andrews made us believe she was. She was a bit of a bitch.

Tomorrow we go home. I'm not ready to leave yet. I just love it up here. Vermont's a really cool place. If only my throat would stop hurting...

CAROL   Saturday, August 5

I think we've been to every Schloss Ludwig ever built. That man had an appetite for castles. One of them, Schloss Herrenchiemsee (which Pennie can actually pronounce), was fashioned after Versailles. Old Ludwig loved Louie. Those two. What a pair! Anyway, we're enjoying the palaces, the shopping, the breathtaking scenery, and the fabulous food.

Today we got lost in the Marienplatz—near City Hall. Where those giant figurines prance around the clock tower. They said it was first performed by live dancers in 1517, to observe the end of the plague. Of course, Pennie and I were just plagued with how to get back to the hotel.

Tonight ended with a formal dinner party, the two of us decked in our evening finery, dancing till blisters bloomed on our toes. I love Germany—ja— but will be glad to get home. I'm starting to miss Maggie.

MAGGIE   August 5

When Aunt Susie and Uncle Phil drove us to the train to go home, my stomach felt like a volcano ready to erupt. I puked while I was getting out of the car. Ugh. Ann had to go back without me. I stayed with Aunt Susie for another day. Then took the train home by myself. I miss Mom.

CAROL   Tuesday, August 8, 9:05pm

Reentry has been a challenge—my life in rural Massachusetts mundane and somewhat boring compared to the thrill of cosmopolitan Munich. I have to make my own friggin' breakfast. Sheesh.

But I was happy to see Maggie. She honestly missed me, and I missed her. No surprise, considering all the souvenirs I brought home with me. Our first contact on Sunday night was so sweet—she sounding genuinely excited to hear my voice when I called her at Rickey's. Such a rarity these teen years. I'm also glad to be sleeping in my own bed.

The excitement has worn off. We had our first fight, over, oh my, the computer and bedtime. She got sick when I was away and we have a big weekend coming up. Damn it! I need to be a mother again, a role that was sweet to step out of for a week or so.

MAGGIE August 8

I'm glad Mom's home. She brought me back some cool stuff from Germany. A gauzy blouse made in Italy that Mom says is very European. And a key chain that yodels. Today we got along real well, 'cept we just fought about.... what else? The Internet! Wow, what a surprise! I wonder if it's worth all the trouble it causes.

CAROL Saturday, August 12, 10:40pm

We're in Westminster, MD for Lauren's wedding. After picking Ma up in NJ on Thursday and driving through traffic from hell, we finally settled in at Days Inn. It's a challenge to be with my family after my European excursion, but seeing my niece float down the aisle on Johnny's arm made the drive worth it.

Maggie wore a sleek new dress, with a pair of 4 inch heels that used to be mine. *Did I really wear those things?* She looked stunning. So grown up. I wore a slinky blue number I bought in Munich and felt divine. Borrowed a pair of Maggie's shoes to complete the outfit. The wedding bells chimed at St. Joseph's in Eldersburg on a magnificent spring-like day.

Maggie sat with Andrew, as both of them were participating in the wedding mass. Lauren and Joe faced the audience. The priest had his back to us—so we could see the newlyweds' faces. A nice touch. Lauren beamed as they sat holding hands. They both seemed so relaxed, so happy, so sure of the step they were taking. Some of us do, some don't. What can I say?

Mag and I danced so much at the reception, the bottoms of our feet ached when we crawled into bed. My heart—brimming with love for my family—is on the verge of eruption.

MAGGIE August 12

Today was my cousin's Lauren's wedding. We had to drive down to Maryland, which totally sucked. We brought Ma down, whose PC monitor is broken.

Mom can't handle it at all. She got pretty bitchy from driving so long, which is understandable. But it's still annoying.

The ceremony was really pretty, but long. I hadn't been to a Catholic mass in a while. My cousin, Andrew, and I took part in presenting the gifts, which was cool. I was honored that Lauren included me. We met Joe's family, who I really liked. His mother, Kathy, made us laugh.

The reception was a blast! Mom and I danced a ton. I also danced with Andrew, which was nice. I hardly get to see him, and I love him a heap. His brother, Matt, too, but he wasn't there. I actually danced with wild Uncle Phil. To "Mambo #5" no less. That was an experience. He's so funny. His girlfriend says he loves to dance, but never does. He should dance more. Everybody should.

CAROL August 14

Sue, Lizzie, and Toni left for Illinois. My heart is breaking. I stayed in bed much of the day. I couldn't muster the strength to drive over to say good-bye. What will we do without them? Oh my gosh. I just realized they're leaving on the anniversary of their son's death.

MAGGIE August 14

Mom just reminded me it's Nicky's anniversary. He died four years ago. When he was eight. Two years after he had the big seizure. They put the wrong size tube down his throat in the emergency room and his brain got all messed up from it. Mom said he went into a vegetative state. I always hated when she said that. He was still Nicky. He was like a little brother to me. I'll never forget one of the times he had to stay in the hospital, and they were afraid he might die, and I just wrote in this little notebook, *Nicky don't die, Nicky don't die, Nicky don't die*, over and over again. Hoping that the words would save him.

CAROL August 17

Ideas are spinning for the Cows manuscript. Should be ready in a week or so to send back to Little, Brown. If they want to publish it, I'll get paid real money as a children's book writer. I can't keep living like this anymore. The money I get from Rickey isn't enough. Thank goodness for credit cards. This could be my big chance.

MAGGIE August 17

I'm so sick of hearing about Mom's writing. She always wants me to read her stuff. I've been doing this job since I was seven, when I worked on a project with her when she was getting her Master's. "The Story of Princess Margaret: A Veggie Tale." About a princess who didn't like to eat her vegetables. She asked me to illustrate the book for her. Of course, we still have the original copy. Mom has revised the story hundreds of times since then. Now called "Yuck and Yum: A Veggie Tale." She still hasn't gotten it published. Surprise, surprise.

CAROL Friday, August 18, 11:45pm

Driving home after dropping my daughter
at her dad's   the week before me slips
open its arms   seducing me with
the breadth of its bare chest....

MAGGIE August 21

Dad and I are spending the week in Lake George, NY. The lake is so beautiful. It's surrounded by mountains and dotted with little islands. This is the first vacation the two of us have taken in years, besides our weekend trip to NYC.

The motel we're staying at is kind of crappy, but it's got a pool, which is the most important thing. I just took a swim and reek of chlorine. Yuk. The motel is right next to this A&W restaurant. It's the old drive-up kind, where the waitresses hang trays from the car doors. It's so cool. They make wicked good waffles. And of course, yummy root beer floats.

CAROL August 22

Just got back from a few days on the Cape, visiting my friend, Joanie, in E. Orleans. She has a gorgeous house that's a short stroll to the sea. We went out to dinner and drove on the beach. And combed the sand for shells and sea glass. I stopped at a ritzy thrift shop on the way home.

How I love the ocean! I need to bath in its essence at least once a year. I must have been a dolphin in another life. Or maybe a whale.

MAGGIE   August 23

Dad said he'd let me practice driving in this state forest behind the motel. I'm so nervous, but excited. At least I have some warning this time. When we were in Hamilton visiting Arlene, Dad just pulled the car over to the side of the road and announced I was going to drive. I thought he was insane. But I drove all the way down to the end of the street, turned around, and drove back. I did really good. But backing up scares me. I hope he doesn't make me practice that. I'm afraid I'll drive the Jeep into a tree or something.

CAROL   Thursday, August 24

I've rounded up Ida Mae and her Cows and sent the manuscript back to Amy Hsu at Little, Brown. I hope she likes what I've done. Once I got into revising, it was fun. It's the days before the writing starts that feel like a dentist appointment.

MAGGIE   August 25

I have "The Walrus and the Carpenter" running through my head. Despite the movie being very trippy, it's one of my favorite scenes in *Alice in Wonderland*, and it's one of my favorite poems.

> 'The time has come,' the Walrus said,
>   To talk of many things:
> Of shoes—and ships—and sealing-wax—
>   Of cabbages—and kings—
> And why the sea is boiling hot—
>   And whether pigs have wings.'

Of course, the movie's version is completely different from the original. I find it so frustrating, 'cause I learned it the Disney way, and it's wrong. That's one of the many reasons it's bad to see a movie before reading the book.

CAROL   Friday, August 25, 11:45pm

Maggie came home after spending a week with Rickey. We began our re-union with a trip to the dentist, which is always traumatic for her. She rebels against dental care, a way to throw the finger at Rickey and me. We saw Sam while we were there. As we left the office, she promised to take better care of her gums—to brush more and floss. Promises, promises. We stopped to see Nicky's tree while we were in the neighborhood.

We also went to the mall for some back-to-school clothes. Ugh. These trips are challenging. I more or less twiddle my thumbs while she searches the racks. I try to stay out of her way—making suggestions is now punishable by death—while still being somewhat available if she wants my feedback. Walking a tightrope across the Grand Canyon seems more appealing.

After buying a pair of jeans, we made a pit stop at home. I gave Mag an early b-day present, a top I bought at the swank thrift shop on the Cape. Swank thrift shop sounds like an oxymoron. But I was happy she liked it. I hesitate to buy her clothes anymore. I've become alien to the preferences of this woman-child of mine.

We went to Pleasant Street to see *Est-Ouest*, a French film with Catherine Deneuve. I thought my daughter, who loves the French language, would approve—bending over backwards is my M.O. these days.

At one point in the evening, Maggie commented on how much we laugh now. I clutched my heart. She's right. We do laugh more. In those first years of recovery, after Rickey left, I was too depressed to even smile. Hallelujah for small gifts!

MAGGIE August 26

We went to see Nicky's tree. The one Sue, Tony and Lizzie planted at his memorial service. Two weeks before I started 7th grade at Hampshire Regional High School. Everyone stood in a big circle around the tree and said what they loved about Nicky. Mom read a poem she wrote. Sue read one of Nicky's favorite books. "*On the day you were born the Earth turned, the Moon pulled, the Sun flared, and then, with a push, you slipped out of the dark quiet where suddenly you could hear... a circle of people singing with voices familiar and clear.*" That year, Mom got a copy for my birthday. It still hurts me to read it.

MAGGIE August 27

I can't get Nicky out of my head. I was thinking about the day we played bowling with him and Lizzie in front of their house. They lived on this dead-end
road in Northampton. So we always played in the street. Sam was there too.
He was a little wild. I actually saw him at the dentist the last time I went. I
didn't even recognize him. If his dad hadn't been with him, I never would
have known.

Anyway, they set up these little plastic bowling pins and rolled this dinky
plastic bowling ball at them. You had to roll it pretty hard to knock anything
down. But every time Lizzie or Nicky hit the pins, they would both dance
around the street. It was so cute. Especially when they'd walk right up to the
bowling pins and toss the ball at them. From two feet away. Sam, he was a
whole different story. He stood there with this wicked devilish look on his
face and threw that ball as hard as he could. And knocked them all down, of
course. We tried to get him to roll it. No rolling the ball for Sam. He wanted
to win.

CAROL August 29

Maggie and I just got back from the Van Gogh exhibit in Boston. Stayed overnight with Lauren and Joe. We were hoping to see his landscapes and still life
paintings.

Rickey and I had stayed in a pension not far from the asylum in Saint-Rémy-
de-Provence, where he painted *Starry Night*. Just being surrounded by Van
Gogh's work made me cry. Like I did with Monet. His water-lilies brought me
to my knees. I sobbed for twenty minutes. Maggie just loves going to museums
with me.

MAGGIE August 29

I really wanted to see Starry Night. It's my favorite of all Van Gogh's works.
But unfortunately the exhibit was only of portraits. I really liked this one
self-portrait he did. It was pretty dark and twisted. Makes sense, though. He
painted for 10 years. Then shot himself when he was 37. I guess he was a
pretty messed up individual.

MAGGIE   August 30

Sorry, oz!

The fish is dead,
I killed him myself.
Murder in the first degree.
He took the long swim.
His grave is shit and piss.
Such is the way of it all.
And I, the one who did the deed.
Will buy a fish tomorrow.
A blue one will be better.

CAROL   August 31

I've been reading a lot about the teenage brain. US News and World Reports ran a feature on it. The part that controls judgment and emotion is not fully developed until the early twenties (and surely gets lost during *The Pause*). In Massachusetts, they let them drive with 'undeveloped' brains. Its motor vehicle department is clearly indifferent to these studies. One could get agoraphobic just thinking about it.

I took Maggie to get her permit. I'm doing fine with it. About as fine as a chickadee in the jaws of a thirty pound alley cat. Afterwards, we rounded up stray decorations from Party World, including a back seat full of helium balloons. Those buggers bobbed around the car the whole way home. A quick stop at the grocery store for a cake and a cart full of junk food, and we were all set for her Sweet 16 celebration. The one with no boys sleeping over! You hear me?!!

MAGGIE   September 1

Ann, Nat, Jack, Jeanne, Chris, Robs, Beth & Marie came to my party. Carrie didn't come because she went to Goth night with her boyfriend. I think everyone was pissed about her dumping us for a guy.

So, eight people were here. We watched a few movies, jumped on the trampoline, and just hung out. Mom wasn't going to let Chris and Jack stay 'cause she doesn't like the idea of co-ed sleepovers. Which doesn't really make sense, 'cause I've slept over Nat's house w/ more guys than that. But 15 minutes before Jack's Dad came to pick them up, I convinced her to let them stay. I was all, there's nothing to worry about, no one will hook up.

Then Chris spent 45 minutes persuading Jack's dad to let them stay. We even wrote a note to Jack's mom, saying, "Nellie the cat will stand watch over the sleeping bodies." Of course, Jack and Jeanne hooked up. While watching *Snow Falling on Cedars* in the guest room. Then Jack accidentally blurted it to his parents the next day. Real smooth. Mom also found out, but she didn't freak out, which I give her credit for. Of course, she's no Peter, who will let anything happen at his house as long as no one dies.

CAROL September 2

I was really nervous about her party. This was the first time Maggie invited boys since she was six. I could barely handle *that*. She sent out twelve invitations, four to boys, and I secretly hoped some of them would turn her down. What kind of mother hopes her daughter's friends have other plans the day of her party? It's been my yearly wish since becoming a single mom. So sue me!

At 5:00, the kids began to arrive. Six girls and two boys, all of them bigger than me. It seemed a manageable sort of number, though my stomach disagreed with the figure. It did flip-flops for most of the night.

The kids were fine. They watched videos, jumped on the trampoline, and wolfed down lots of junk food as the hours rolled along. These parties are important to Mag. Her friends are great for celebrating birthdays. I smartened up this year and invited some of her friend's moms, who stopped by in intervals, keeping me sane for some of the night. At 11:00, after folding myself into an easy chair with novel in hand, dear Maggie, who has the nose of a bloodhound, sniffed out my fatigue and pounced for the kill. "Please, oh please, Mom, it's the only time I'll ever be 16. Please can't Jack and Chris stay over." *You hear me?!* Who am I kidding?

MAGGIE September 2

I must still be tired from my party. I just walked by the guest room and got freaked out by the doll. The one Mom made for me when I was eight. She was as tall as me back then, straps on her feet so you could dance with her. We used to call her Molly. Now she just lounges on the chaise in the guest room, in her leopard jeans and Mets' cap, and scares the crap out of me when I walk by.

Wow. I can't believe I'm a junior this year. It seems like only yesterday that I danced with Molly.

CAROL Sunday, September 3

I had dinner with Belle at Cha3s. It wasn't good. We're both really needy right now and it never works when we are. She did most of the talking, while I listened. And stewed. It came out sideways. I told her I couldn't listen to her stuff about Brodric anymore. She needs a real therapist. Just like my mother did.

CAROL Tuesday, September 5, 10:55pm

I gave Maggie her last birthday present, a surprise I'd planned for a while. Mike took us for a ride in his 1917 Model T.

After our jaunt, she practiced driving. She had trouble coordinating the clutch, accelerator and gearshift today. I had to get us out of the driveway. This continued to be a problem at stop signs. I had to take over halfway through our practice run. I didn't do well as instructor, with Commander *Pause* and her troop of sleep-snatchers invading my room at 4:00 this morning.

This time of year always feels bitter-sweet to me. Although I'm eager to have the space for writing, I miss Maggie when she starts school.

MAGGIE September 5

Well, school starts tomorrow. Good-bye vacation, hello hell-hole. Joy!

Mom got our neighbor to take us out in his Model T as a belated birthday gift. Mike got his T in 1939 when he was sixteen. It was *way* cool.

Yeah, I'm sixteen! I've got my permit! I drove Mom's car. Stick shift sucks. I'm not good. It made Mom nervous. She's not a very good driving teacher.

But she's a good regular one.

I made popcorn later on and I wouldn't share it with her 'cause I was in a bitchy mood. Though, I usually do. If she wants some, she should make her own. But I could have shared. I was just being a bitch. That's me!

CAROL Monday, September 11, 9:57pm

I hate everything about my life. I hate being a single mom, hate being a writer, hate being poor, hate my age, my looks, the aches and pains that have moved in to stay. The list goes on ad nauseam. I'm not certain what set me off. It doesn't help that I haven't heard from Len since I got back from Germany. Or that Dell sent me someone else's repaired computer instead of mine. Or that I couldn't decipher the damn ballot when I voted tonight. Grrr.

It was probably the conversation I had with Mag. I've been uptight about money. Spent too much this summer. I've been talking about it a lot, something she heard excessively after Rickey left. She lectured me about getting a real job. "I mean, why bother having a Master's in Education if you're not going to use it," she roared. This came directly from her father's mouth. I made sure to mention it.

I reminded her, "I started my Master's when I was six months sober, just four months after your dad flew the coop. I was terrified. Being here for you was primary to me, so going back to teaching made sense at the time." She rolled her eyes. That didn't stop me. "I wanted to have the same hours and vacations as you. But that was no way to pick a career," I said, groveling, "though I'm sure it's very common for single moms." Maggie stared out the window.

I continued to argue my case and said, "I've always been there for you."

"Yeah, Mom, except when I had to be the parent all the times you cried." The truth of her words were like a dagger through my heart. I crawled to my room when we got home, crashing to my bed, sobbing. Maybe that's why I hate everything about my life tonight.

MAGGIE September 11

I think Mom and I played some version of brutal truth tonight, 'cause what I told her was the truth, and it was brutal. Hence, the name. This entire year Mom has only been writing. Her only source of income was unemployment checks. I've pretty much ignored all this, but lately Mom has been mentioning how we are strapped for cash. A lot. And I really don't want to think about this, 'cause then I'll go back to where we were 5-6 years ago, when Mom used food stamps, 'cause her only job was subbing.

But it wasn't until this summer that she started looking for work again. And she hasn't worked at the library for a year. She's been depending on unemployment and money from Dad. And her writing. Which pays shit. She says she wants this dreamed up part-time job, with flexible hours so she can write. And she hasn't looked for anything else. I just think it's incredibly selfish. She has this Master's degree that she won't use, and she's just sitting on her ass at home.

She told me she has put all herself into taking care of me the past ten years, like it's this big sacrifice. She's my goddamn mother! She's supposed to. Mom just needs to realize until her stories start making some real money, she needs to look elsewhere. And she's put so much into this writing thing of hers, saying we'll use the money for college. And go to France like I've always wanted. What if it never takes off? We're once again left with shit. And a bunch of broken promises. Grow up, Mom.

CAROL Thursday, September 14, 10:22pm

It was good to take a break from my writing and ride my bike the five miles cross-town to retrieve my car. I did the same yesterday after dropping it off for repair. A year and a half after the accident, my car is finally fixed. I left a message for Len at his office. Why hasn't he called me? Payback for flirting with Joe.

I also got an upsetting email from Belle, which left me unsettled and crabby. She's really mad about my asking her not to talk about her marriage problems. Has threatened to leave our friendship. I feel shaky and scared, but can't listen anymore. My need to be true to myself is really strong. At some point, I'll write her a letter and try to work things out.

Mag helped with dinner, something she's done for the last few weeks, and critiqued my driving as I whisked her to driving school, a fun (not) new facet of her teenage job description. I was in no mood to have my imperfections pointed out. Again. I wanted to rip her tongue out.

I miss Sue. We never got to hug goodbye.

MAGGIE   September 14

Ah…. Driving school is over. I mean, I enjoyed the class, but now it's one less thing on my mind. Which I need. But driving lessons start soon. Should be fun.

I walked home from town hall. Actually, I had walked halfway when Mom stopped for me. It was only about a mile, but I had never walked it before.

I had drama today, which is why I had to walk. We're doing three plays! One is *A Midsummer Night's Dream*. Yea! I love Shakespeare. "Oh what fools these mortals be." But that's not till spring.

First, I'm gonna be in *The Children's Hour*. Debbie pulled me aside to explain the reason why I didn't get the lead. She wanted me to play Mrs. Tilford, the antagonist of the story. Except Debbie said she has to be played as if she's doing horrible things for the right reason. I guess Debbie thinks I can do a good job of finding that balance. Yeah, I'm feeling good now. I might not have the lead, but I have the most difficult part. Note to self: do not let this go to your head.

The whole play is going to be a stretch for all of us. Ann and Carrie are going to be playing the two school teachers. And Ann's character falls in love with Carrie's. And I ruin it by being a bigoted bitch.

CAROL   Monday, September 18, 10:10pm

I linger online past midnight, picketing bedtime, knowing I'll be roused two or three times before dawn. Woken by those rollicking troops from hormonal hell—the ones that stomp through my friggin' room four times a night—and broadcast the change that's plaguing my existence. It's really screwing up my life. I hate myself these days.

Today I scheduled a lap-top swap with Airborne Express. I'd finally get my computer back and return the one owned by the Colorado man who has mine. They never showed up.

Maggie paid the price when she got home.

She wanted the last bag of kettle corn, her new favorite snack, which I'd eaten while she spent the weekend with Rickey. While she searched through her cache of snack food, I mistakenly chuckled about having it all to myself.

She went bananas. She dove for the cupboard and seized my stash of chocolate—a plastic heart of assorted goodies—containing a bon-bon gifted me by Len, which I'd been saving for a dismal day. Like today! Always the cool Mom, I went ballistic—trying to snatch the chocolates away from her.

We joined in a cat fight—our claws extended—scratching each other like felines in combat. For a brief moment, I was able to observe myself engaged in this shameless battle.

MAGGIE September 18

171 more days. It's pretty bad. I'm already counting down the days till school gets out. This is not a good sign.

I was exhausted when I got home today, so of course, I took it out on Mom. But she does that too. Takes her stuff out on me. We got into this huge catfight (her words) over food. Popcorn and chocolate. A lethal combination. So first the cat fight, and then we just yelled at each other for an hour, off and on. I disappeared into my room for a while to escape, but it doesn't always work.

Damn, I need a lock!

CAROL Tuesday, September 19, 10:25pm

I'm feeling pressure about money. I'm using my credit card way too much. Maggie's dumping on me the other night didn't help. I get controlling when I'm overwhelmed or scared. Maybe Maggie's right. I need a real job. Shit. I have two real jobs. I'm a single mom and a writer. Another item on the menu of being me right now.

Adding a spritz of kerosene to the day's mixed grill, I hit Mag with news of wanting to put our cat to sleep. Right here at home. Have a little kitty service for her. My timing was sketchy. She didn't take it well.

Nellie is old and seems fairly miserable most of the time (the pet doesn't fall far from the tree). It took Maggie two years to agree to put Rusty to sleep, our dear Chocolate Lab. I may have a long haul ahead of me.

MAGGIE September 19

Tonight Mom brought up the idea of putting Nellie to sleep. I was the one who suggested it in the first place, but tonight wasn't good timing. She said I'd have to go with her to the vets, which I SO can't do. But Nellie seems like she's in pain, and well... she's almost 17. The first word I ever said was "Nennie" (Nellie).

Follow-up to the entry: Our beloved Nellie died on her own in February, 2002.

CAROL Sept. 20

They say the truth will set you free. I say it's downright mortifying.

MAGGIE September 20

What the hell has happened to Mrs. Meyers? She was nice to me and Nat for about a week. Now she's such a witch. Yells all the time. She wasn't like this when we had her for French. And all the damn papers we have to do for her. At least one a month. Honor's English sucks.

CAROL Thursday, September 21

I need a wife. Badly. And a husband. Maybe a man servant would do. This house is a mess. The dust balls are taking over. I can hear them rolling around at night.

Cripes. There's no food in this fucking place. I'm starting to sound like Maggie.

MAGGIE September 21

I think everyone should have a list of things they want to accomplish in their lives. Or things they just want to do for the hell of it. I've got a working one going right now.

- See the Great Pyramids
- Learn to ski
- Have a one-night affair that leaves me w/no regrets

- Drive a Porsche
- Find my soulmate
- Finally tell off Teresa
- Have Olivia and Ethan
- Go bungee-jumping. Or sky-diving
- Establish a career that is both successful and fulfilling
- Fly somewhere completely on a whim
- Visit Matt and Becky in Panama
- See the Taj Mahal
- See all of Western Europe, Japan, New Zealand, Australia, St. Petersburg, Brazil, and Venezuela.
- Meet Prince William (and make him fall in love with me, of course)

chapter four

Give Me a Break!

MAGGIE   September 23

Wow. My birthday party is having repercussions I never even thought about. How the heck did I forget about Valerie? Nat and I spent months becoming friends with her, trying to make her fit into our group. And we didn't do it for Jack. She's such a nice girl. I just love her. But I totally forgot about her after Jeanne and Jack hooked up at my party. Didn't even occur to me that he cheated on her. And now the shit has hit the fan. And Jeanne is being painted as Mata Hari or something.

CAROL   Sunday, September 24, 11:18pm

Seeing a movie tonight   a foreign
flick you'd probably like....
*   ... Suddenly   the sky splits*
a seam ~~oozing~~ and oozes bushels
of water   pattering to the
pavement   and people scamper
as raindrops bounce off asphalf like
ping pong balls.   A ~~funky~~ tie-dyed shirted
woman   nuzzled ~~the~~ freckled cheeks
into her ~~young~~ lover's neck   spraying

kisses around his ear.   I can only
glimpse ~~for~~ a moment   any
longer would be ~~sheer~~ torture
remembering what it
feels like   yearning
for a drizzle of
your love
sometime
soon.

Cripes, if Maggie doesn't stop bugging me about the co-ed sleepover thing I am going to scream. Or jump off a bridge. Or better yet, push her off. Good Gak! Will you please drop it already!! And Len dahlin'—when the hell you gonna call?

MAGGIE September 24

Co-ed sleepovers. It's amazing the things Mom and I fight about. And it's amazing how this stereotype of teenagers having sex all the time has been drilled into the minds of parents. I mean, sure, Jack and Jeanne hooked up. But that was an anomaly, and it's not like they were banging each other right in front of us. Wake up, Mom! In two years, I'll have guys sleeping in my dorm room. What's the big deal?

CAROL Thursday, September 28

Greg is pushing back the deadline for the book. He promised it would be released on my birthday. Now he says February. His life as a homesteader is a priority. All this aggravation for 30 copies of the book. That's it. No other pay. Grrr.

I mean, so far I've made $300 for my essay in Salon and $75 for "My Father's Ashes." No wonder Maggie's so mad at me. I need to get a book published that pays real money.

And I'm not doing well with disappointments. I need to let go of expectations and access my Buddha self. With all the damn food I'm stuffing down, it shouldn't take long.

MAGGIE   October 2

I'm going to be sick, waiting to be picked up for my first official driving lesson. Doing driving class was easy. This is the real thing. And I think I'm gonna puke. *Why aren't they here yet?* I hope Sheila's not with me today. She's terrifying. The driving instructor from hell. And my English paper's due tomorrow. Oh crap. Hester Prynne and feminism. Ugh. Where's the toilet?

MAGGIE   October 5

I've added to my list of things I want to do.
   - Go on a safari in Africa;
   - See Tibet, Fiji, and Hong Kong;
   - See every state in the USA, even the boring ones.

CAROL   Monday, October 9, 10:47pm

Columbus Day weekend—a long one with Maggie. Took a dose of Ignatia. I've been crying on and off ever since. We planned to see *The Exorcist*. One of my all-time scariest movies. It's been re-released for its 25th anniversary. I cringe at how quickly that half of my life whizzed by.

When the movie was over, I wanted to go to Bread & Circus. Maggie flipped out. She didn't want me to go and threw a teenage temper tantrum to prove it. We yelled and screamed at each other in the car, then carried it into the store. She followed me in. Here we are in this whole foods grocery store—where people practice serenity while shopping, with peaceful music playing to help them along—and we're in the middle of produce haggling over how long I'd get to shop. Maggie's complaint being I say I'll only be 15 minutes, then take 45.

She's had it with my gross exaggeration of time. I wanted to run away from her, but she wouldn't let me. It must've been the movie we saw. She was surely possessed.

On the ride home, I admitted my part for Maggie's anger with me. Again! She was right. I do misjudge the time. Truth be told, I tell her what she wants to hear.

MAGGIE October 8

We got into this big fight in B & C about how long she would take. I was yelling at her in the middle of the store. It was great! She was really embarrassed, which was the purpose. I got her really pissed.

CAROL Wednesday, October 11

My period comes whenever it damn well pleases. Twice in one month, zilch the next. Last year every two to three weeks. I've had it up to here. When I was in high school, we used to call it the curse. I always found that offensive. Not anymore. When it shows up these days, that's exactly what I do.

MAGGIE October 8

For some strange reason, I've been thinking about sex recently. Not that I want to do it or anything right now, because basically I don't know anyone I'd really want to have sex with. Except for maybe David Boreanaz. Or Prince William. The boys at Hampshire Regional are such dorks. I would not want any parts of their bodies inside me. It would just be wrong to be w/someone I've known since kindergarten. It would feel like incest or something.

MAGGIE October 15

Louise, Marie, Jeanne, Jack, Joe, Mel and I were all hanging out at Nat's last night and Peter called to say he was on his way home. Of course, he didn't know we were all there, so we decided to make up these signs on poster paper saying: WELCOME HOME, PETER. Like we were throwing him a welcome home party. It worked, sorta. He didn't buy the whole welcome home party, but at least he didn't get mad at us for being there.

CAROL Monday, October 16, 10:40pm

Heard from Greg. Still no word on the poems he will finally use. I asked him to cover the book in purple. He's searching for just the right shade. He always thanks me for my patience. If he only knew how little I really have!

Swimming in a sea of
impatience   I breast stroke
the days   bobbing ~~around~~
through waves of ~~utter~~
disbelief   each sweep
of ~~my~~ *arm   pushing through*
billows of doubt
treading in an ~~sea~~ *ocean*
of anticipation
stopping   now and ~~again~~ *then*
floating a nigh   the
faltering me.

What the hell! It took seven years to get a divorce. What's a few more months for the chapbook!

MAGGIE   October 18

I am so tired of my friends putting me in the middle. How did I get assigned the role of mediator? Is it because I've known Jeanne the longest? I'm the only one willing to be compassionate about how she's feeling. Doesn't mean I don't resent my part. And my friendship with Valerie is down the drain. But really, what other choice could I make? It was between someone I've known since I was five and a girl I wouldn't even be friends with if she hadn't started dating Jack. And since that's Jeanne's job now... my loyalty is with Jeanne. I just wish Nat would back off. She's really giving Jeanne a hard time about breaking up Jack and Valerie. And Carrie is too. It must be from her history with Jack. I think she still feels hurt from him breaking up with her.

CAROL   Sunday, October 22, 9:40pm

Exhausted. What else is new? Went to Vermont to visit Sui and Phil. To celebrate my birthday with people who don't sneer and growl at me for breathing. I wanted Maggie to go, but she said a friend was having a party she didn't want to miss. I just found out the party she didn't want to miss was the one SHE had while I was out of town.

I should have known. She insisted on knowing exactly when I'd be leaving and when I'd be coming home, things like that. Uh, isn't that a part of *my* job description? I questioned her about her concern. She assured me all was well. I chose to believe her. I lied to my parents—most teens lie to their parents.

I found out by mistake. I called Ann's mom. Ann had supposedly gone to the mythical party with Maggie. About to thank her for transporting Maggie to *that* party, she beat me to the punch and thanked me for letting her daughter spend the night at my house. Well, what do you know about that? It sure explained all those weird conversations the week before.

And the fact that Maggie vacuumed the house while I was away. Come on now. If that ain't no big-butted red flag, I don't know what is!

MAGGIE October 22

It's weird. I still remember this poem about kindergarten I wrote in sixth grade. It must be 'cause Jeanne was here last night.

> As I look inside myself,
> I see,
> Laying on the desk,
> A half colored,
> Orange pumpkin.
> I press down,
> Too hard,
> Making my hand hurt,
> I wished
> That pumpkin
> would disappear....

Is it actually possible Mom doesn't suspect anything?

CAROL Monday, October 23, 9:40pm

Mag and I just had a fight. I'm having trouble settling down. We haven't fought like this in a while. After the day I had, it was really upsetting. Who am I kidding? It's always upsetting.

When I talked to her about the party, she admitted having friends over, just two, then finally confessed to having a party planned while I was gone. I'd done the same in high school, at my folk's summer cottage, and the damage was far worse. I was scrubbing up beer stains and vomit for what seemed like weeks. It kept me busy while I was grounded.

She claimed it's the only way she could have all her friends sleep over—including boys, which seems to be acceptable for some families these days. This single mom is not one of those families. Makes me way too nervous. I don't want one of Maggie's friends getting pregnant under my roof. Although, I really don't think Maggie's friends are into big time sex. Yeah right. I also didn't think she'd throw a party while I was away.

This teen stuff is so confusing. No wonder teenagers are flummoxed. (I love that word!) Their poor bewildered parents are so mixed up. At least, I am. This is when I REALLY hate being a single mom. So tonight, I will dream about the Mets thrashing the Yankees in the Subway Series. That will surely ease my anxious heart.

Dream on, you fool.

MAGGIE   October 23

Mom's really pissed and says she can't trust me. But the main reason why I was having the party was so my guy friends could sleep over. She refuses to talk about coed sleepovers. She goes on and on about how it's too hard being a single parent, yada, yada, yada. And when I talk about Peter, who is *also* a single parent, who lets Nat and Chris have coed parties ALL THE TIME, she gets all pissy. She's all like, "I don't care. Don't talk about him." She shouldn't use single parenthood as an excuse. Some of these guys are my best friends, and she won't let them stay. It's not fair.

CAROL   October 24

I'm really starting to hate Peter.

CAROL Thursday, October 26, 11:15pm

I'm watching the Mets/Yankees game while I write. I need to do more than witness this gruesome battle between the arch rivals of my youth. I've loved the Mets since high school. And hated the Yankees…well, since then.

Each game comes with this undercurrent of sadness. Maggie was two the last time the Mets played in a World Series—Rickey and I were wrapped in Mets madness. We both love the game. Okay. Enough already. Stop thinking about him! I think I just might puke.

Those damn Yankees just scored two runs in the ninth. Grrrrr.

Let's Go Mets!!

MAGGIE October 26

Carrie's dog died, and Ann's grandma person is dying. Poor Mrs. Aidan. Ann's known her since she was little. There was lots of crying today. It's so unfair. I'm sticking by my motto that life sucks.

CAROL Friday, October 27, 11:15pm

We celebrated my birthday tonight. Ate at a Japanese restaurant that Maggie suggested. One of her friends wants to practice law in Japan someday. And me, well…I'm just a minion to my daughter's whims.

So I reserved one of the private dining rooms for us. We sat on the floor, with our legs dangling in a chasm below the table. We ordered sushi, which Maggie even tried. She's getting more venturesome, nibbling on Wasabi and ginger slices, as well as slurping a bowl of miso, with little cubes of tofu dancing around.

The food was mediocre. The room was too isolated for the occasion. And the bill gave me heartburn. I'm so aware of my money mismanagement these days, which bruised the festive nature of the night.

MAGGIE October 27

Still no decision on what's going on with coed sleepovers. Dad seems to be on my side, but Mom wants to wait until we talk with our therapist again. All my friends have had a sucky week. I'm still pissed at Jack for screwing Valerie over, but he and Jeanne seem really good together. So I'm caught between being happy and angry. Ack... this is too confusing.

CAROL Saturday, October 28, 10:48pm

It's my birthday. I did not hear from Len. Bad move. What's his freakin' problem?!!

I peel your picture from the
fridge   and imagine snipping
it into minuscule pieces   then blast
ing the stereo   as I gleefully
stomp all over the scraps   or
maybe I'll just torch your
thing...

I love the image.

MAGGIE October 29

Efil

this
is
such
shit.
fuck
it
all.

CAROL Monday, October 30

I wonder if I've made a mistake. Telling Maggie she needs to get to know herself before she gets involved with a man. No. It's important.

Teenage stuff. So confusing.

I decided to call Susan, so we could work on this coed sleepover thing. She didn't call back right away. Thought she might be mad, from all the shuffling I've done with our last few appointments. Had to be my fault. Until she called tonight. Oy vey! I scoff at my lack of trust.

MAGGIE October 30

Could I really have another paper due for Meyers next week? On Monday? Freedom and Society in Huck Finn. Bah. I hate her.

CAROL Tuesday, October 31

I'm having trouble with trust. Trusting myself, trusting the process of life, trusting the universe will take care of me. So much to trust, such little time to learn how.

MAGGIE November 1

I don't know how it happened, but the whole Jeanne/Jack thing has finally become a non-issue. Maybe it's because they really do seem happy together, and that's allowed everyone to get over it. I know it has for me. And I haven't really seen Valerie at all, so there's the whole "out of sight, out of mind" thing working too.

Except w/Carrie. She isn't getting over this. I stayed over at Nat's the other night and Carrie cut my hair for me. While she was doing it, we got talking. She didn't say why she can't let it go, just that she can't. I'd say it was some hang-up left over from her own relationship w/Jack, except she's w/Dingle now. So that can't be it. I just don't know. Thankfully, they hardly have to interact w/each other. It's a good thing Carrie is doing duel-enrollment at Greenfield Community College this year. It cuts back on the possibilities of them getting into it.

CAROL Thursday, November 2

Amy Hsu from Little, Brown returned "The Day the Cows Got Loose" and asked to see a second revision. YAY! But I'm not sure how to fix it.

I think I can, I think I can.

CAROL Friday, November 3, 11:18pm

Mag and I saw Susan today. I said I thought things were going well between us, that we were re-negotiating our relationship. The constant bickering of the last two years seems to have waned a bit.

Maggie told Susan her side of the party story. And then I dropped the bomb. I said we will not be having anymore coed sleepovers. It's too much for me to handle as a single mom. And even though I'm fairly sure Maggie's not sexually active, I can't count on her friends. Let them fornicate like we did, in the back seats of cars, I thought to myself. I bit my tongue.

Maggie was upset—she couldn't yell at me as usual, so tears filled her eyes. She said she felt angry and frustrated. She sounded so clear. I felt proud of her, though guilt was my prevailing feeling. I held my ground and didn't waver on the issue. I tried to elicit support from Susan, asking how other parents felt about this issue. She said most parents wouldn't let their teenagers attend a coed sleepover—much less have one in their house—with a very small portion not caring what their kids did and another small portion fully trusting their kids. I felt supported by her explanation, but still tasted the slimy guilt on the back of my tongue.

Maggie hadn't resolved her feelings by the time we left. She was still mad and walked 20 paces ahead of me. I felt like the villain in every Disney movie we'd ever seen. We stopped by Turn It Up, a used CD boutique in Northampton—an oasis for the angst—and by the time we left, Maggie seemed to be okay.

We went home and watched *Free Willy* and had a decent night together. Part of me sensed Mag was relieved by my decision. I might just be kidding myself. Anyway, score one for the Mom!

What the heck's up with Len? He did this when we were young. Disappear for a while. Some things never change.

MAGGIE November 3

Mom and I went to our therapist today. And it really helped our situation. Oh wait, no it didn't. She refuses to even compromise when it comes to coed sleepovers. She just doesn't want to be liable if someone has sex and gets pregnant. Yeah, sure, like that would happen. That just doesn't happen, at least with my friends it doesn't.

I was so mad when we left Susan's. The anger was a huge bubble inside me, ready to explode. Instead, I kept my cool and chose to shop for CDs, rather than be around her. Shopping—the cure for what ails ya'.

CAROL Saturday, November 4

I called Len. To give him hell for missing my birthday. His damn voice always makes me melt. I hate that about him. I love that about him. It's a handicap. I can't stay mad for long.

I asked if he was seeing other women. He said no, then read me a poem he'd written about helicopters. He can hear them before anyone else detects their sound. A product of his time in Vietnam. It made me cry. We are inching our way towards seeing each other again. Maybe Thanksgiving at Sui's. Next time we talk, I'll propose it to him.

Is he telling me the truth? I don't think he's seeing anyone else. I just think he's scared.

CAROL Monday, November 6

Talked to Amy Hsu from Little, Brown about the revision. I'm still not clear. Have to call Leslie. She'll help me with this.

Egad. Tomorrow's election day. Please, oh please, anything but George Dubya.

CAROL Tuesday, November 7, 11:05

Like the rest of the world, Maggie and I wait for the results of the presidential election. This political turn of events is almost as exciting as the Subway Series. I feel at home with this uncertainty. Reminds me of growing up in the '60s. It's also a way for Maggie and I to connect.

We share many of the same political principles and philosophic values. I've actually learned a lot from her.

As we watched the news together, seeing a clip of Palm Beach voters protesting like we did in our twenties, Mag said, "Mom, let's move out of the country if Bush wins the election." I reveled in her earnestness.

"Where should we go?" I said. "Maybe somewhere in France? We'll live there for four years. It'll make up for your missing French IV this year," which made her laugh.

"No, I was thinking about Canada." The haven where her friends talked about moving. Her friends are so important to her now.

I envy this time of her life. Such a passionate phase. I remember it so well and long for times I can rekindle that fire. It happens when I listen to Motown music, the feelings so palpable I can't do anything but dance. The uncertainty of this election also fuels that in me. Sparks some passion. It feels good and I think my daughter recognizes this. It takes us out of the tedium that often flavors our days. It reminds us of the importance of justice. I've raised a daughter like myself, which makes our fights fierce at times. But I'm glad I've given her my strength and determination. Goddess Bless America.

MAGGIE   November 9

Tuesday was election night, and we still don't know who's president. Vice-President Al Gore (D: idiot) and Gov. George W. Bush (R: bigger idiot) are running.

It's this whole big deal because Bush was going to win, then Florida had to recount its votes. And that's the deciding state.

It's funny, Gore is winning the popular vote, but Bush is winning the electoral vote. In other words, Bush may win, even though more people don't want him as president. Bush is a bumbling idiot, who I despise. A lot of people I know are threatening to leave the country if he wins. Nat's Mom wants to move to England and Lynn's Mom wants to go to Canada. Josh wants to take over Guam and make it Canada 2. I want to move too. He'll totally screw up our country. The biggest problem is Bush is pro-life. Not good for women. These people are going to affect my future. And I am sincerely afraid.

CAROL   Monday, November 13

Sent the *Cows* back to Little, Brown. It's out of my hands. I just hope this is it. That my first children's book gets accepted for publication. Now stay away from those fingernails.

MAGGIE November 14

Saturday Night Live had this special called "Presidential Bash 2000." It was a collection of their best political skits, and Mom taped it. Today we watched it in history class. We've been following the election pretty closely and Mr. Brouchette thought it would be a good break to have before the recount. God, was it funny.

Jeanne and I immediately latched onto Al Gore's 'locked box' line. "Well, Jim... Rather than squan-der the su-plus on a risk-y tax cut for the weal-thy, I would put it in what I call a... "lockbox." And Larry spoke in Bushisms for the rest of the day. *Strategery, dignitude, inockurate*—stuff like that. Most of the kids in class are Democrats, so the anti-Bush skits were a big hit.

I felt a little embarrassed by the quality of the tape, though. We don't have cable. Everything was a little grainy.

I swear if Bush wins, Nat and I are moving to Canada.

CAROL Friday, November 17, 11:48pm

I am up to my elbows in financial fears. Diving head first into that murky pit of distrust.

After learning of a health insurance increase of $120/month come January, Maggie slaps me with a $90 petition. The chorus field trip and high school yearbook are dueling for my check book.

The money I get from Rickey isn't enough (of course, he and Teresa think it's way too much). I need to get a freaking job. If I do, I'll have to give up my writing. If I give up my writing, I'll be miserable. If I'm miserable, Maggie will be miserable too. Crap, I hate this.

We'll have to keep living on credit. I'll pay it off when I sell the house. I want to be available for Maggie—now more than ever—something that was impossible when I started recovery. I was a vacant store front, waiting for the owner to restock the shelves. Maggie would tap on the door, gaze in the windows, but no one was there. She played the mom most of the time. She deserves to have a full time mother. I'll hand over the money stuff and pray for its timely arrival.

MAGGIE   November 18

Oh god, they're back. The damn lady bugs. Everyone I know is always like, "Oh, you're so lucky. I'd love to have lady bugs in my room." Ha. One or two might be okay, but I have twenty. Every winter it's the same thing. They swarm my ceiling. One just peed on me or something. It smells horrible. And that smell seems to draw more of them out. I need the vacuum. Suck 'em all up. That'll teach 'em.

CAROL   Sunday, November 19

OH MY GOSH!! Pennie has offered to give me money—to be my patron—to help support my life as a writer. OH MY GOSH! Am I worthy of this?! How will it affect our friendship?! Will she have expectations I won't be able to meet?! I'll worry about that later.

OH MY GOSH!!!

CAROL   Sunday, November 26, 11:10pm

Maggie's been with Rickey since Wednesday, while I spent Thanksgiving at Sui and Phil's with Len. His kids were with their mom. He told me he was drinking again. Just the occasional glass of wine. For special events. Of course, I freaked out when he told me this. He wasn't drinking when we first started dating. It was one of the attractions—aside from the chemistry we've always had—it made me feel safe. I told him I won't be with him when he drinks. He agreed not to drink when he's with me. I wonder how long this will last. I need to go to Al-Anon.

I'm more aware of what I do when I get close to someone. I get scared, then do stuff to push them away. Nit-pick and argue. Getting close to a man without the aid of alcohol scares the shit out of me. Maybe it did the same to him. Every time I see Len, I worry it will be the last time. That I'll screw things up someway. Maybe I shouldn't see him anymore. Damn alcohol!

MAGGIE November 26

Mom got back together with Len. She waited three months to hear from him. I just think it's a little sad. She should've found someone new.

CAROL Monday, November 27, 11:40pm

Maggie was genuinely happy to see me when she got home from school today. All smiles and hugs. We discussed our separate celebrations, then she retired to her cave to check email, and agreed to help me flip the trampoline at 4:00. She returned willingly and persuaded me to jump with her before upending it for the winter months ahead.

While I watched a deeply moved Oprah Winfrey interview Nelson Mandala, Maggie went back online, promising to help with dinner at 5:30. Much to my surprise, she strolled into the kitchen at 5:35 and helped make the pizza I planned for this evening. We chatted and played.

She said, "I missed you, Mom." Tears pooled my eyes. This is something she only says after my saying I miss her first. The obligatory, "I missed you too, Mom."

Monday is our designated TV-dinner night. We opted for a movie and couldn't agree on which one to watch. Something new to fight about. She talked me into *The Princess Bride*.

Both of us relish its comic satire. Though I felt grateful for this time with her, I was fully aware, this will not last.

MAGGIE November 27

School started again, after a five-day break. I was exhausted when I got home from Dad's, but Mom and me still got along. Probably because I hadn't seen her in four days. We made pizza together. Whoop-de-do. Bonding. Joy. I'm more concerned with my friend's relationships. They're disintegrating before my eyes, and I can't do anything to stop it. I really hate being powerless.

It bites.

CAROL Tuesday, November 28

Driving back ~~home~~ to Massachusetts
you toss me a question   "do you
ever think   you try too hard?"
and the confusion from it   swirls
around the ~~pit~~ center of my chest.
Seeking truth   I dive   into a sea
of self-helpers   that navigate the
bookshelves of my room   swim~~ming~~
ming through   fathoms of pages
treading on a swell   of
competent words   until
I find   the line   that shouts
an answer.
I am more vulnerable
with you   than I've ever
been   before   in my life…

MAGGIE November 29

It's interesting. *The Grapes of Wrath* is both depressing and inspiring. Tom Joad lost everything, yet he continued to go out of his way to help others. Of course, I'm never going to find out how it ends, because Mom won't leave me alone. I need to concentrate on what I'm reading. Ack! Have to do better on this paper. If I cross my fingers and wish really hard, is it possible for her to stop breathing? God, I hope so!

MAGGIE November 30

She's still breathing. Damn.

CAROL Saturday, December 2, 12:19am

I got nine hours of sleep last night. A major miracle. Coming on the heals of a satisfying week of writing, including five finished poems, an essay, revision of "It's Not Fair," and the poetry manuscript I submitted to Perugia Press. Writing is a way of life for me now. I'm not myself when I'm away from it for any length of time. It's still hard for me to believe this is who I've become.

When Mag got up at 12:30, we planned our day. She'd changed her mind about attending a concert at Pearl Street, opting to stay home with dear ol' Mom. I was glad. I bought the makings for Chinese dumplings, the pot stickers we get when ordering take out. I was looking forward to some time with her. We've not yet found our rhythm in the kitchen. I'd still like to get a sense of cooking comfort with her.

We agreed to meet in the kitchen at 4:30, then go to the mall afterwards to get Mag a pair of shoes. I'd been struggling with some old issues after meeting with a career counselor. How I've always felt ineffective in my work life and in my relationships with men (things I also told my first therapist). I felt upset because of it. I had trouble with Maggie's attitude toward me, which basically means treating me like a stupid shit. Her specialty when she's tired. As a writer, I'm open a lot, like a child, feeling naked and exposed and vulnerable to attack, which makes it hard to be around her assaults towards me. Today was one of those days.

I could feel my body tense up and when I'm tense I get curt and controlling, which doesn't go over well with Maggie. Or anyone. I wanted this cooking gig to work, but Mag was more concerned with shoes and kept nagging me about going to the mall. She does the same to me I did to my mom—bugs me 'til I say yes. I have trained her well. I now refer to it as harassment. She seems to grasp the terminology, but doesn't necessarily stop the behavior.

So I opted for bribery. Told her if she helped me finish the dumplings and held off her snide remarks, I would take her for a new pair of shoes. Hey, you do what you gotta do!

MAGGIE   December 2

Well, it's official. There is no way Carrie and Jeanne's friendship will ever be fixed. Carrie told me herself. As I said before, this sucks.

And Mom is stuck on using the word harassment. To quote *The Princess Bride*, "I do not think it means what you think it means." She freaks out whenever I ask her anything more than once. Okay, so I nagged her a little about going to the mall. But then she bribed me. I had to keep my mouth shut or only say nice things to her while we made these stupid dumplings. But hey, new shoes are new shoes.

CAROL   Thursday, December 7, 11:45pm

Greg sent the list of poems. There's only 16. I'm sure he told me 22 or 24. What's going on here? And the sequencing—I don't think it's right.

This chapbook means people will read about my divorce. Do I really want that?

Emptying a tattered carton
of pea soup   not quite
thawed   into a blue
white   and red   cool~~whip~~
whip plastic   which settled
on a shelf in the fridge ~~which~~
housing shriveled whipped
topping from lack of use
I notice flecks of burnt
soup   scraped from
the bottom of the kettle
some the size of quarters
frozen inside the ~~defrosted~~
defrosted lump.

Thinking of the weekend
I concocted the soup
~~poring~~ pouring over books

I'd already drunk and
stewing about the final
outcome of my divorce

I stand and wait ~~as~~
as the micro wave zaps
the charred pieces
and wonder if
it will taste like
my marriage
burned   beyond
repair.

I've read the letter five times. Taking in his editorial notes is mind-spinning. I will read it again tomorrow. And another five times I'm sure. Can I really make the changes he wants me to make? I do like the poems he picked. To celebrate, I had me some pea soup for lunch.

MAGGIE   December 9

Nat used to have one of those big make-up Barbie dolls. The kind that are life-size from the shoulders up. I say *used to* because last night Chris, Jack, Mel and Joe put it out on the deck and lit it on fire. It didn't really burn. It just kind of sat there and melted. And left a big hole in the deck. Peter freaked out when he came home from his girlfriend's. We could hear him screaming at Nat and Chris from down in the basement, where we were hiding. It was bad. But funny.

MAGGIE   December 10

This year was my turn to pick out the tree. It took a while to find a good one. There's not many left since Stanley died. I think the Howard's have stopped caring about the farm.

When I was little, I used to take my mittens off to test the needles. If you couldn't go back and forth on the branches, the tree was no good. Ouch. It hurt too much to decorate. So that's the tradition. Check the tree for prickly needles.

Mom even wrote a book about it. At the time, I thought it was kinda' cute. Now I just think it's weird.

CAROL Monday, December 11, 10:25pm

I feel a strong resistance to journaling right now. My psyche pleads for vacation. Must be pressure from the season. God, I hate Christmas. Can't they move it to another time of year? When I have more energy. Maybe celebrate it in May? I'll have to write to the Pope about this. I needed to rant and rave. So I fought with Maggie.

It started over a chair. My lazy-girl. She wanted to sit in it. I asked her to move. She refused, so I went ape. That bottled up rage came spurting out like a shaken soda. All over Maggie.

She got scared. She dug in her heels. It made me freak out. I tried to unearth her from the chair. Not once. Not twice. Four freakin' times. 'Twas not a pretty sight. I knew I should get out of there, but shit, I wanted to kill her. I finally yanked myself from the room. Tore into the kitchen. And returned too soon. Threatening something so lame, my brain's deleted it. Maggie felt sorry for me and gave up the chair. Thank goodness one of us can be an adult.

Afterwards, I conceded to watching *Pretty Woman*. It's not one of my favorite movies. It was the least I could do. I'm just thankful I made it through the night without a felony.

MAGGIE December 11

Mondays bite to begin with and this one just topped the cake. Mom totally freaked out over me not moving out of her recliner. I mean, she completely spazzed out. And because she made such a big deal about it, I couldn't give it up. I was being really stubborn, just to stick it to her. Mom resorted to trying to kick me out of the chair by tilting it forward. I didn't budge.

But this was a freak out to end all freak outs. I hate being stuck taking all Mom's crap. It's times like this I wish I had a sibling, if only to get some of her stuff. Somehow, we actually managed to watch a movie together an hour later.

CAROL   December 12, late

Sometimes   I find
myself   staring at my
daughter   wrapped in the
warm ~~red~~ vermilion of our
couch   adolescence blooming
on her snow white chin
eyes   ~~fixed~~ straight ahead
curly black lashes
reaching thick Irish
brows   knitted in concentration
nose   slightly turned   like the elves
who fashion Santa's toys
mouth   as full and
succulent   as the leaves
of the jade ~~plant~~   that resides
on a shelf   cornered
in my room.   I am
a robber   stealing
the hope diamond   or
crown jewels   the richness
of this moment   as priceless
as the yearly budding of
my Christmas cactus.

MAGGIE   December 12

Mom's determined that I will have some idea of how to cook before I leave for college, and I'm finally willing to learn. Making a cheese soufflé together on Christmas Eve has become a tradition, and earlier this year we conquered sweet and sour kielbasa. A recipe I got from Teresa. My cooking abilities have been broadened from pushing microwave buttons. Yay me!

CAROL Wednesday, December 13

I'm freaking out right now. I'm just not sure I can fix these poems with all that's going on this time of year. I need to write back to Greg, but I'm putting it off. Not sure what to say. I also get sad during the holidays and looking at these poems, well… it just makes it so much harder.

MAGGIE December 13

God. Mom just told me about her abortions. I'm not sure how I feel about this. I mean, I am strictly pro-choice. So that's not the issue at all. But I could have had an older brother or sister. Maybe one of each. Then again, if she had these other babies, I may never have been born. She might have been satisfied with just having them. Then, no me. It's kind of weird thinking about Mom that way. I wonder if anyone came with her to hold her hand. I forgot to ask her.

CAROL Thursday, December 14, 10:25pm

Mag had a snow day. The fluffy stuff fell like the dickens. Millions of tiny flakes and none of them look the same. So amazing. I'm reminded of another snow day, but those days of sliding in bed next to me are long gone. Sigh.

My daughter   slid   into my bed
this snowy morning   and ~~she~~
snuggled close   to my fear.
I was glad to breathe in
the calmness ~~that~~   she wore.
Suddenly   she picks up
the phone   and requests
the number for school
cancellations.
I reveal the digits
with an air of why
in my tired voice.
She looks at me with quiet
disdain and casually says   Mommy

you've been such an airhead
I just need to make sure.
I shrug off the shame ~~and~~
and tell her in my most
motherly voice   that I'll
not forget to cook for her
or wash her dirty clothes
or figure out her math homework
or tuck her into bed at night.

She smiles   and
cuddles close to
to my sobering
strength.

She came back from Rickey's well rested—and so was I. She said she thought of me while she downloaded *Cabaret.* I played Sally Bowles in a UPenn production 25 years ago. *"Mama, thinks I'm living in a convent, a secluded little convent, in the southern part of France...."* Sally's opening number. It was great. *"What good is sit-ting alone in your room... life is a Cabaret old chum...."* Maggie still has my T-shirt from the show.

She wanted to tell me something. But hesitated. Said it was corny. I egged her on. "Mom, it's just that I respect the way you chose to live your life. You weren't afraid to try things."

My hand aimed for my heart. Tears crowded my eyes. I asked her what she meant. She said she respected my involvement in theater, and how I traveled around the world, and that I stopped drinking. There were parts of my being a writer she didn't like, but she respected me for doing something I cared about. That I loved to do. I was so moved. Words cannot describe how I felt. But I waited on her the rest of the night!

MAGGIE   December 14

The Supreme Court decides the election. Fuck this shit. Democracy my ass.

oink

pigs.
the raging masses.   whose ideals mean shit without the proper i.d.
starvation without representation.
want want want.   need need need.
since when are these synonyms.
who are you, if you don't consume.
peace on earth, good will toward men.   don't forget the women.
and children.

where's your good will now?
gotta protect you and your own.   fuck those who get trampled in the riots.
god bless the ole u. s. of a.

CAROL   Saturday, December 16, 3:19am

I had this weird dream. Len and I were staying at this house, on a cliff, house-sitting for someone. The bedroom had a glass wall overlooking the ocean. The sea was dark and furious. There was a thunder storm going on. Huge bolts of lightening streaked the sky. A storm so bad it woke me up. I'll have to ask Belle what this means. Scared the daylights out of me. Need to go back to sleep. Please let me sleep again.

MAGGIE   December 18

Mrs. Meyers is the worst kind of teacher. Today she handed back our *Grapes of Wrath* papers. She gave almost everyone in the class a D. And then she started yelling at us, saying had we learned nothing in her class yet and that we were the stupidest class she's ever had...*the stupidest class?* Come on. I'd say that's a really horrible way to motivate students.

CAROL   Tuesday, December 19, 11:19pm

I wrote to Greg about "DIVORCE PAPERS." I'm sure he'll think I'm a pain in the butt. "These poems are so personal—this is so much harder than I ever expected. Would you consider this sequence: On Mother's Day, Curled Corners,

Sometimes, Repairman, Sheild Dissolves, Holiday Weekend, The Sheriff, Hearing #1, Oh My Gosh It's Brian, Hill, Cuddles Close, After Hearing #2, Finishing Divorce, Remarriage, Only Love, Spring Fever, Without My Daughter. I realize it throws off the seasonal progression, but can this possibly work for you?"

I added this too: "I was also wondering about the number of poems. It appears we're back to 16. I realize you chose a few of the longer ones, but I'm wondering if you'd consider using two or three more to bring the page count up to 25. I thought we'd agreed on two dozen poems." I also thanked him for searching for purple paper for the cover.

I just hope I can fix the poems. Egad. I've never done this before. He wants me to cut some of my words. I can't tolerate anymore letting go.

chapter five

Not Some Druggie!

CAROL   Monday, January 1, 2001, sometime in the middle of the night

I am *so* freaking tired. The damn *Pause* is wrecking my life. I made merry with Len last night in New London. I've been sober for 11 years. Our time together got off on the wrong foot.

Arriving at the hotel   I ~~inquire~~ ask
at the desk   unsure if you are
here   and she rings the room
handing me a phone   and I hear
a ~~ice~~ chill in your voice   wondering
what sits behind your icy tone   then realize
you ~~are~~ may be mad   I left you stranded
at the ferry…

Oops.
*   …I imagine ~~that~~*
you longed for ~~my~~ arms wrapped
tightly   around your   shivering
torso   as ardent lips   pressed
a welcome mat onto
your mouth.…

I guess that's what happens when you miss my birthday!

Now please, oh please, Commander *Pause*. Call back the troops, so I can get a little sleep.

MAGGIE January 2

The Art and Artistry of Handholding

It doesn't have to mean anything. You tell yourself this every night.
It might mean nothing.
But it is the not knowing that is killing you.
Your ability to read people has gone the way of the dodo bird.
Birds fly south for the winter.
Bears hibernate. You wish you could sleep away the next three months.

It's not the sleep that's killing you, it's trying to sleep.
The wondering keeps you awake.
It drives you to question things you wouldn't usually question.
Even if you knew the answer, you wouldn't know your response.
It's too complicated.

You get a sick feeling inside when you think about it.
Does that mean you are frigid, incapable of emotion.
But that's not what worries you.
Are you incapable of arousal. Are you frigid that way.
What could possibly be worse.

And you don't know if it's him, or you.
If you had the chance, would you take it.
Or would you dance around it like you have, avoiding any possibilities.
In fear of discovering the truth
Is ignorance bliss, or the lesser of two evils.

Your nails are all chipped.
Continue on this way, and you'll never get the chance to find out the truth.
The truth wouldn't want you.
And that's the worst fear of all.

CAROL Wednesday, January 3

I remember when I first got sober—I was this vast wasteland. Ding dong, no-body home. My marriage was an endangered species, verging on extinction. I worked my sorry ass off to save it. Did the steps in record time. Renee asked me, "Are you trying to be the star of AA?"

The transformation from who I was when I drank versus who I was after stopping was dramatic. I tried letting go of old behaviors—perfectionism, people pleasing, stuffing feelings, indirectness—before I had anything to replace them with. Tried to recreate myself. More accurately, to recover myself. I was afraid to leave the house sometimes. In a way, Mag and I grew up together. She held my hand, while I held hers.

MAGGIE January 3

The Gatsby paper's due in 2 days. The book is really fascinating. Fitzgerald had a very cynical view of American society. Gatsby wasn't great; he was an incredibly flawed individual. The book ends on such a sad note, that Americans are chasing a dream that can never be reached. "So we beat on, boats against the current, borne back ceaselessly into the past." Fitzgerald considered changing the title to "Under the Red, White and Blue." I think he should've. It fits the theme better. Two days. Shit.

CAROL Thursday, January 4

Got a postcard from Greg. He's wondering where the poems are. Shoot. I better send those babies back tomorrow.

MAGGIE January 8

The play is this week. God I hope I know my lines. *"There is no relief for me, and there never will be again. I didn't come here for that. I swear to God I did not. But what I am or why I came doesn't make any difference. Doesn't matter. All that matters is you and—you now. Help me, Karen."* I don't want to let Debbie down. Or get laughed off stage. Shit.

CAROL Friday, January 12

Got a nice letter from Greg. He said the rewrites read very well. And my sequencing makes sense. He wants me to change a line in "Remarriage."

Driving home from school
a dawdling voice   divulges
her dad is getting married
that's interesting   I say
I'm glad you told me
I say.   Not good to hold
those ~~kinds of~~ things in.

We're quiet as we pass
the pond   noticing swirls
of rippling grass   shouting
green   beside the ~~tan~~
tawny stub of cornfield
embracing its border.

As we pull in the drive
she confesses of the bridal
shop they browsed
to find an imposing gown
for the occasion   how
nice   I say   slamming
the car door.

She retrieves the mail and
flings it on the kitchen table
ready to unload more nuptial
treasures.   I turn to her   with
a quiver on my lips   and whisper
I need years to myself....

CAROL Saturday, January 13

Went to see Maggie's play last night. They're doing *The Children's Hour*. Debbie likes to pick the heavy-weight productions. Maggie's playing the grandmother, Mrs. Tilford, and did a great job, if I say so myself. At'sa my kid. Sui and Phil came down to see it with me.

It's funny—Greg went to the same high school as Maggie. His favorite teacher and mentor is also Maggie's favorite—Mr. Mercus.

MAGGIE January 14

Carrie has turned into such a sex fiend. Seriously. She is going at it every chance she gets. Even when we're all at Natasha's. She and this weird guy she just started dating named Steve, were going at it on the futon upstairs. I feel so bad for Dingle. They broke up, and she immediately starts banging this other guy. But I guess the sex must be pretty good. 'Cause she never stops. Go Carrie. If it's that hot, why not do it? I wonder what my first time will be like.

CAROL Monday, January 15

The holidaze (as Palmtree calls them) suck for me. I do it all. Cut down the tree, drag it home, put it up, throw on the lights, decorate the house, buy the presents. It seems endless. This year I struggled getting back on my feet. With "DIVORCE PAPERS" due out soon—these poems are so revealing—it may be a while before I get my balance back.

Day off from school. Had a huge fight with Mag. We're crawling the walls here.

MAGGIE January 15

No school today. I *almost* wish there was, so I could get away from Mom. Couldn't the weather give me a break? At least if it was nice out, I could get out of here and go visit Ann or Nat. But no. We're in the middle of winter. A wicked icy winter. Good thing I'm planning a trip to NYC over winter break— to see *Rent* with my friends. It'll be so much fun and I'll get a much-needed break from Mom.

CAROL Tuesday, January 16

I started a young adult novel today. Felt good. Been wrestling with my writing routine for a while now. I'm thinking of calling it *Amelia and Bessie*—after the great aviators.

Amelia has always known the truth. Face it. The truth has a way of whittling at your bones and gnawing on your heart. And though she hauled it around like a sack of manure on a hot summer day, she kept it to herself. Just like her mother, she kept it to herself. Until the day he came back. A day that split open the sack and let the shit out of the bag.

MAGGIE January 24

Meyers is such a bitch. She really is the *worst* kind of teacher. Who not only criticizes you, but does it in front of the whole class. But today she went overboard, even for her. She made Jeanne cry. Poor Jeanne. Who dragged her pained ass into school after having her wisdom teeth removed. And what's the first thing that happens to her? Meyers lays into her about her paper not being well written. Does the woman have no compassion at all?

CAROL Thursday, January 25

Snowing outside—floating in space—see Rickey shoveling. I really am losing it.

I made hot chocolate and we watched *Willie Wonka* again. Movies are our safety net—a way for us to be together, without my worrying about trespassing on her life. Afterwards, I gave her a foot massage—feet sore from new boots—and lounged in her room 'til midnight. We chatted like girlfriends, kindhearted energy flowing between us, which comforted me. These moments are worth millions.

MAGGIE January 25

Oh god. What can I do with my life if I don't go into marine biology?

CAROL Friday, January 26

I talked with Len. It was bad. Bickering over when we'd see each other again. We do this a lot. The down side of a long distance affair. My need for affection is far greater than his. He still gets plenty from his kids.

I drove Mag and her friends to see *Chocolat,* then went back home to write. Maggie stayed the night with a friend, giving me lots of space to work through my angst and finish a chapter on the new book.

CAROL Sunday, January 28

Hanging up the phone   after
chatting with my mom   I want
to seize our conversation   and
place it in a jar   one of those
twelve-sided All Fruit beauties
I save   and ~~then~~ *I'll set it on the*
top shelf of my refrigerator
knowing   I will take it out ~~tonight~~
later in the day.   Opening the
lid   I'll nestle the rim to my ear
the sweetness of my mother's
voice   swirling inside   her
lilting words   a cherished
lullaby....

Last night, Mag and I made pizza, working side-by-side in the kitchen like it was an everyday event. We watched *The Thomas Crown Affair,* while munching on our culinary creation—feeling blessed to have this simple night in our lives.

She felt lousy this morning. I gave her a dose of homeopathic Chamomile which brought her back. A walk around the reservoir with Pennie did the same for me. Then we schlepped our butts to B&N for some tasty treat, more girl talk and loads of laughs. I can always count on Pennie to make me laugh. One of the funniest women I know. What would I do without her?

Afterward, I endured some Super Bowl at Mag's request and finished the night making a birthday card for Ma. It's a dear time for us. We're having more good days than not and I'm grateful for them all.

MAGGIE January 28

Ah, I love three-day weekends. Especially when Mom and I are getting along. Last night, we watched a movie together and talked about Mom's experience with drugs. It was weird. It's really hard to picture my Mom doing drugs, discounting alcohol, of course. I have to admit, it bothered me when she confessed she smoked pot pretty much up to the time she stopped drinking. Which was when I was five. That means she smoked when I was alive. My mom should not have been doing that stuff. She's my mommy, not some druggie. That's not her.

MAGGIE January 29

I think this is the best way to keep your kids from doing drugs. None of that "Just say no" crap. DARE doesn't work. Just tell them about your own experiences. I'll never do acid, because I don't want to flip out like Mom did. Ed gave Mom and Merry some acid one night and took them into NYC. They sat in Penn Station and watched the people walk by. Their passing faces changed with each hallucination they had. Merry and Ed thought it was funny. Mom freaked out. Then they had breakfast at some dive in Times Square at 3:00 in the morning and the place got so hot, Mom had to run outside. Of course, it wasn't the restaurant. It was the acid. That was it for Mom. She begged them to take her home. She had flashbacks a few months after too. Seeing things that weren't really there. That's some freaky shit I want no part of.

CAROL Monday, February 5, 11:53pm

I'm meeting Rickey at Friendly's on Wednesday. To discuss college plans for Maggie. I hope the restaurant's name inspires us. He's so singled minded about her college search. Sees the price tag as the most crucial element. I'm dreading the encounter.

MAGGIE February 6

I told my friends I'd organize our trip to NYC. I've been online all night trying to get tickets. It's not going well. Shit. What have I gotten myself into? I can't get any for winter break. What if I can't get the tickets? My friends are depending on me.

CAROL Wednesday, February 7, 10:30pm

Amy Hsu from Little, Brown left a message and I called her back. They liked what I did with "The Day the Cows Got Loose" and are trying to get Lynn Munsinger to agree to illustrate my picture book. I'm psyched. She said they'll bring it to the publication committee soon. It's the group who makes the final decision in the acceptance process. If they like it, they'll buy it. It felt good to bring that information to my appointment with Rickey.

Our meeting went well. As soon as one of us said something negative, the other put on the blinker and changed the direction. We even hugged good-bye. A successful conference. We may even be back on the same team. Not if Teresa has anything to do with it.

MAGGIE February 7

I wonder if Nat can drive us to NYC. But what if she can't? Then what'll we do?

CAROL Thursday, February 8

Mag says Nat's driving them to New York. I don't think so. Crap. I have to let go of her. How the heck do I do that?

MAGGIE February 8

The Great American College search has begun. Since I'm half-way through my junior year, it's time to start looking. I've wanted to go away to college, far away, but unfortunately, I live in the 5 college area. Some of the best liberal arts schools are less than an hour from me. Including Hampshire College, which I am seriously considering. Problem is—tuition for Hampshire is $35,000 a year. So Dad's pushing UMass, where I SO don't want to go. But that's what the big 'meeting' was about between Mom and Dad. My parents get together about once a year to compare notes. Mom gets all nostalgic and Dad is all "Mr. Freeze." And all "your money problems are all your Mom's fault." Of course, Mom does that too.

But the real purpose of this meeting was to attempt to prove they are raising me together. Of course, they're not. They've spent a good half of my life blaming each other for their problems. That's not going to change overnight. But it does make me sad to hear Mom say she'll always love Dad in some way. 'Cause I have never heard Dad say that. Truth is, I'm pretty sure it was Dad's fault my folks split up. He's the one who still drinks and smokes pot and who I think had an affair. It makes me sick. How do parents expect kids to turn out okay if they can't fix their own lives?

Untitled (1)

father's musIc saturates life.
but worst, motHer's.
pAin feeds into me, inTo meaning.
lovE billy joel (this night is mine),
k.d. lang forbidden—destroYed hOme.
even with ice skaters: tUrn ice wars.
oh, pretTy woman.
the crime, two-fOld, lasts forever.
raDio is pain. he is pAin.

p.s. where is mY massage?

CAROL   Friday, February 9, 11:40pm

Mag and I had a good night. We got online to do a financial aid search and filled out a scholarship application. Became silly in the process. It was fun to laugh with her. She rarely laughs at my jokes. Thinks they're lame. Then I feel hurt. I take the things she says to me too personally—sad, but true. Except tonight, I was in a good mood—after a month-long holiday funk. Being back on track with my writing makes things better for us.

We also drove to the library to research colleges—we're serious now. She has started having doubts about majoring in marine biology. "I don't think I'm passionate enough about it, Mom." I did this. Told her to follow her passion. Now look what I've done. We looked for schools that include it anyway.

While we were there, Mag ran into Beth. She invited her to the sleepover at our house tomorrow. I'm not a go-with-the-flow kind of Mom. When it comes to these teen parties, I'm thrashing upstream with no life vest. All those raging hormones in one place submerge me in worry. Tomorrow night, I will be a fragrant petal floating down a peaceful brook.

Dream on, precious petal, dream on.

MAGGIE February 9

This college major thing is really bugging me. The decision feels so final and so big. It's been drilled into us that the decisions about college and a major are the most important ones we'll ever make. I know I could change it when I get to school, but I don't want to have to do that. It would disrupt things too much. So I have to decide now. But if it's not marine biology, what do I do? I've been *so* sure for *so* long, I don't know if I can change my mind now.

MAGGIE February 10

Ordered 6 tickets for *Rent*. Yay! Of course, they're not as good as I wanted. They're way in the back. But we're all together. Which could have been a problem. I can't believe we're going. This *really* rocks. But how're we gonna get there? Nat can't drive. Peter says *no way* she's driving their car to NYC. This is getting wicked complicated.

Shit. Better clean up. My friends will be here soon.

CAROL Sunday, February 11, 9:45pm

The sleepover was very low-key. All my worry for naught.

Mag's working on getting tickets and transportation for herself and five friends to see *Rent*. 250 miles away. Am I really okay with this? Maybe I should go with them. No, I have to let her do this. How can I let her do this? She's only 16. She could get mugged or raped or… oh god, Carol, stop it.

Tonight we saw *Crouching Tiger, Hidden Dragon* at Pleasant Street. Maggie and I have different viewing styles. If something strikes me a certain way or confuses me, I may lean towards the person I'm with and whisper a comment or question. Not Maggie—who most would say has better theater etiquette than her mother. She stares at the screen, eating popcorn and sipping soda. But tonight her reaction really pissed me off. At one point, she told me to shut-up, then later on shushed me.

Teacher comments on my grade school report cards were varied, but always included the word chatty—what can I say?

But what really got my goat was when I asked to have the rest of her popcorn, which I knew she wouldn't finish, because she's one of those annoying people who stops eating when they've had enough. She not only turned me down, but proceeded to toss that uneaten bag of lavishly buttered popcorn into the trash bin as we left the theater. She's lucky I didn't pull a George Costanza and stick my hand in and pull it out!

MAGGIE February 11

Mom and I went to see *Crouching Tiger, Hidden Dragon* tonight. It was a really good movie, but Mom kept talking. She always does this. "Blah, blah, blah." Never shuts up. And when I told her to shut up, she got mad at me. For the rest of the night. And also, because I wouldn't let her have the rest of the popcorn. She had an adult temper tantrum. She's such a spoiled brat.

CAROL Monday, February 12

I feel so needy. Too much to deal with. The poems, the picture book, Len, Maggie, my friends. The house, the bills, the future—oh god, the future! Stay in the day, Carol, just stay in the day. It all freaks me out. Can't do it. Shit. I hate this. I need a frigging wife. No wonder men get married. Better yet, I need a meeting.

MAGGIE February 12

Maybe we should take the train to NYC like Dad and I did. $76.00/RT from Springfield. Ack! Who can afford that?

CAROL   Tuesday, February 13

Greg sent me the mock up of the collection. The shape of the book is beautiful. He runs a letter press, setting each letter of my poems by hand. Master of a dying form. He wants me to look for mistakes. It's tricky with the white space I use. He sets dialogue in italics. I love it. As Greg says, *the most graceful manner to set the reader's mind to hearing voices.*

MAGGIE   February 13

Louise & Connie said the train from Springfield is too expensive. Maybe we could go from Hartford? Crap. This is too much. I wanna resign as chair of this trip!

CAROL   Wednesday, February 14

Valentine for Len. My muse.

You are an oasis   the color
of peaches in morning sky.
I'd like to ~~taste~~ bite into your juicy
nectar   savor the succulence
of your fruit   as   it drips from
the corners of my mouth.
I long to bathe in the scenery
of your smile   lingering in
the portal of its expectation.
I yearn to slither into the crook
of your voice   curl my spirit
around your tongue   suck
on the ~~heat~~ fire of your intensity
but more than that   I want
to spend ~~just~~ one precious
moment   wrapped
in the luster of
your mind.

MAGGIE   February 14

Valentine's Day sucks.

MAGGIE   February 21

There's something so incredibly comforting about watching Disney movies. I've been sick with the flu, which bites, 'cause it's vacation. Nothing distracts me from feeling like I'm gonna die like *Mary Poppins*, or T*he Little Mermaid*, or *Dumbo*. Though, *Dumbo* makes me cry. I just hate the flu. I spent all last night puking. Then dry heaving. Kill me now. But after Julie Andrews sings.

CAROL   Wednesday, February 21

My poor baby's so sick. Up half the night with her. Can't wait to hit the pillow.

CAROL   Monday, February 26, 9:35pm

Met with Len in New London. Our favorite place to rendezvous. I was in a playful mood. Had fun teasing him. He brings out the girl in me. At one point, I laughed so hard I fell into the closet. And the love-making—don't get me started—is divine.

A phone call interrupts our rapture
and we are flung from bed by its
~~rage~~ ire.   Missed check out by an hour.
We hustle with our stuff   yours
taking only minutes   mine a tad
more   and as I pack   I cram grief
into the bag with my belongings…

…Driving to the ferry   I ~~propose~~ suggest
the diner   sausage and eggs
to mitigate my woe   and as
we're leaving the restaurant
a favorite song wails through
~~the~~ speakers and I long to dance.

As quickly as words waltz
through my lips   your arms
swirl around me   pulling
me close to your core
doing so much more
than link sausage
ever can.

Len does not like PDA's. That was a pleasant surprise.

MAGGIE   February 26

Just got our *Rent* tickets in the mail. March 10, baby. YEA! I also found out that Ann's Dad is going to New York with us. God! One of the bonuses of this trip was going alone. We're 16 years old! Give me a break! Mom wouldn't even do something like this.

CAROL   Tuesday, February 27

Mag just told me Tom's going to New York with them. Phew. Let him be the bad guy.

MAGGIE   February 27

Ann says her dad will drive us down to Stamford so we can catch the train to Grand Central Station. It'll save us some money. But he will *so* not be sitting in the same car with us. No way! Ann said he'll just hang out in New York while we do our thing, then we'll meet him for the train ride back. What can we do? It's the only way he'll let her go with us. I guess Mom's not so bad after all. What am I saying? Yes, she is.

CAROL   Wednesday, February 28, 10:17pm

Len called to connect. He's growing on me. What does this mean? Just stay in the day, Carol! I found it difficult today. Not hearing from Amy Hsu about my book sent me reeling. I am not good with this waiting. I was anxious and crabby when Mag got home, who was also depleted from her day. After watching

GL, she got online, while I revised poems about the weekend. I opted to make breakfast for dinner. Scrambled eggs with cheese, sausage links and rye toast is becoming a culinary mainstay. By the time dinner rolls around, my creative energy is consumed.

After dinner, Mag invited me to her room, to listen to music and help with a history project that's due. She needed a picture of Rosie the Riveter. I ransacked the Web. Found a good image. She produced a great collage to turn in. We went back online, hunting for prom gowns, listening to more music and had fun. I sensed from the time she got home she needed my company, and at this point in our lives, that always feels good.

MAGGIE February 28

I am so tired. I've had SO much work this week. Two papers and a test. I think my procrastination is catching up with me. I'm completely wasted. And it's only Wednesday.

Mom & I just spent the evening hanging out in my room, listening to the music from the show. It was fun, 'til I reached my limit on quality time. Then I made her leave. Only so much patience in me for mother/daughter bonding or something like that. But it was nice to be with her and not fight. That's a rarity.

CAROL Thursday, March 1

Whatever happened to those good ole' days when I loved to cook? To the passion I felt about food? I believe it flew out the damn window when I became a single mom. Cooking's just another chore of the day. Macaroni and cheese—the best I could do. It was Mag's favorite for years. But I'm thrilled she's eating eggs. She'll eat 'em till she starts clucking.

MAGGIE March 2

Only one week till New York, baby! Eeh! We're going to see *Rent*! Eeh!

MAGGIE March 3

Last night, the guys set off firecrackers in Natasha's wood burning stove. Not a good move. Especially since Peter was home. Mel and Joe ran downstairs with us and hid in Nat's bedroom, while Chris and Nat were getting reamed out by Peter.

CAROL Monday, March 5, 1:20am

It's late—really late for me. Mag and I had one of those sterling nights. Neither of us wanted it to end. So we stayed up.

The rest of the day didn't go well. I got the nerve to call Amy Hsu at Little, Brown. The illustrator they wanted for the Cows turned it down. Crap. And they still haven't taken it to the publication committee as she said they would. She wants a strong illustrator on board before she tries to sell it to them. I wanted to fling the phone across the room. Then wrap the cord around someone's neck. Been waiting ten years for one of my kids books to be accepted. I've never been this close. The tension is brutal.

Maggie saved the day. Rickey dropped her off at 3:00 and by dinner, we were in sync. I played *For Baby* on the guitar for her. Could it be having Len in my life has made me want to play again? I used to sing that John Denver tune to her when she was little. *"I'll walk in the rain by your side, I'll cling to the warmth of your tiny hand, I'll do anything help you understand, I love you more than anybody can."* When I finished, we listened to Mary Travers' version. Maggie said, "Mom, you sing it much better than she does." A rare gem spouting from my teen's tongue. Which quickly turned my day around.

MAGGIE March 5

I am definitely not getting what Mrs. Meyers wants on these damn papers. Why aren't I getting this? I so hate Natasha, who actually does.

CAROL Tuesday, March 6, 1:20am

A huge blizzard cancelled school two days in a row. I whipped together our new comfort meal—scrambled eggs, sausage and toast. We dined with *Hillary and Jackie,* a movie based on the life of cellist, Jacqueline du Pré, which we both enjoyed. We also had a cookie casualty!

We finished the evening in her room, listening to more songs from her childhood, reminding us of her dad. *Stand By Me* was one of his favorite songs. We used to watch the movie of the same name when he lived with us. We called it the 'boy movie,' in honor of the cute cast of young boys. The three of us would cuddle on the coach, eating popcorn, feeling close, with Rusty, our Chocolate Lab, by our side. When I hear the song, I get homesick for that time. My heart cracked wide open being with her tonight. One of those treasure-chest times one dreams of repeating, knowing full well, you can't.

MAGGIE March 6

There's a big snowstorm going on now, so school was cancelled!! Yay! Mom and I spent the evening hanging out. We watched this movie called *Hillary and Jackie*, which was rather depressing. Something Nat would probably like. Mom and I made chocolate chip cookies. Okay, so Mom made the cookies and I ate half the dough. Anyway, Mom made two trays, but dropped one of the trays. I laughed, until I saw how upset she was. She hardly ever makes cookies anymore and half of them broke. She got really upset and I felt *so* guilty. But it was weird, 'cause not only did I feel guilty for laughing, but also I felt guilty for Mom dropping the cookies, which I had nothing to do with.

Later, I downloaded a couple of songs Mom and I listened to when I was little. Peter, Paul and Mary's, "For Baby," which Mom played on her guitar the other night and used to sing to me as a lullaby. And "Baby Mine," from *Dumbo.* Whenever we used to watch that movie and that song would come on, I'd sit in Mom's lap and cry. I was afraid I'd lose her, like Dumbo lost his mom. But it felt good to reminisce with Mom. We don't do it that much.

CAROL Wednesday, March 7, 10:45am

Can't stop thinking about last night. The words to "Baby Mine" drifted around the room like photos in an album. Maggie lost me for a while—not physically, but emotionally—during my early recovery and through the divorce. Will I ever let go of that guilt?

I was so angry and scared back then. It consumed me. I had no idea what it meant to be calm. Like a geyser ready to spurt. I feel grateful for this time with her now. Although calmness is still not one of my strengths.

MAGGIE   March 7

Dad stopped playing "Stand by Me." The last time I remember him playing it, he danced with Teresa. I ran out of the house in tears. It's our song, not theirs.

CAROL   Thursday, March 8

Oh my gosh. It's him. I don't believe it.

Maggie grew up watching *Reading Rainbow*. For seven years, we rarely missed an episode. I was always curious about Larry Lancit, one of the show's producers. Could it be the same Larry I played with on St Cloud Ave. in West Orange?

I called Lancit Media Productions and got his number. Then called his home. I spoke with Cecily Truett, his wife and co-producer. I introduced myself. "Oh Carol, " she said. "I know who you are. You're the one who got Larry into all that trouble when he was young. Your name comes up at family dinners all the time." I couldn't believe what I was hearing. We laughed and talked about the time when I was six and got Larry to help me pull up the freshly planted flowers in his neighbors garden. When my mom was hospitalized again.

I told her about my 'prospective' picture book project with Little Brown. She suggested I fax the text to Twila Liggett, executive producer of *Reading Rainbow*.

I sent the manuscript to her and held my breath all day. I'll dream about my book on *Reading Rainbow*. First—it has to be accepted by Little Brown.

CAROL   Friday, March 9, 11:55pm

Mag's at Ann's tonight, leaving from there for NYC. Gulp.

I spent the evening with Belle and Brodric. We saw *Beatlemania* at the Calvin. It was just what I needed—a night of Beatle music, dancing in my seat to their songs.

But B & B got into a fight. Their marriage is dangling by a tress. They are my parents revisited. I hate being around it, which has become an issue in my friendship with B. She complains about him like my mom did about my dad. I hated it then and hate it now. Seems like she can't stop herself. It's wearing on our friendship. I'm not sure what to do anymore.

Mag will be okay, they will be okay—please let them be okay!

MAGGIE March 10

I finally got to see *Rent*. After two years of waiting, Ann, Louise, Connie, Nat, Carrie and I went to New York and saw the play. It rocked! I never realized how much is lost on the soundtrack. The sexual subtext is missed because you can't see the dancing. But it's a beautiful production.

Afterwards, we wandered up Fifth Avenue. *Fifth Avenue!!* Did lots of window shopping. Prada, Gucci, Tiffany's, Saks 5th Avenue. *sigh* Stopped at St. Patrick's. I took this great picture of the corner of the church. The wall of the church on one side and a glowing red 666 on the other. It was weird. Like a representation of God and the devil. We also popped into FAO Schwartz and played w/giant teddy bears.

I suggested we take the subway back to Grand Central Station to meet Tom. We got on the wrong train and ended up in Harlem. 125th Street (thankfully the train stopped in Harlem). We were totally freaking out, except for Carrie, who thought it was cool. A big adventure. When we got off the train, one of the first things I noticed was, my friends and I were the only white people on the platform. The thing that bothers me is that I was bothered by this. I hate that it was the first thing I noticed. As I'm writing this, I realize this is probably the way black people have felt for centuries: that of being in a place where you sense you're unwelcome. It's a terrible feeling.

CAROL Saturday, March 10, 12:05am

Maggie's in New York. Instead of worrying about her, I spent the day fretting over my call to Larry Lancit. And my fax to Twila Liggett. I just moved my fear from one place to another. Whatever, it worked.

Mag called from the city at 9:00. They took a subway to 125th instead of Grand Central. She was okay and I actually took it in stride. What's happening to me? She asked to stay at Ann's again and could I deliver some extra clothes. I did not hesitate to oblige her, even though I knew she had two papers due on Monday. Decided not to butt in. The new me.

MAGGIE March 11

I am so exhausted. Don't know how I'll ever get these papers done. At times like this, I wish I weren't in the damn honors program. And that I wasn't such a procrastinator. Oh well, suck it up and get the work done.

CAROL Monday, March 12

She asked for a shoulder massage before she fell asleep at 7:00. I gladly agreed, then crawled into bed around 9:00 and was just drifting off, when I heard her call me. I thought I was dreaming, then heard her pleading voice and knew this was for real.

A bit disoriented, I tottered into the bathroom. Her head was hanging over the toilet bowl. It felt like old times—when she would kneel by the toilet for hours, nauseous and trembling—and not wanting to be held for comfort.

She wakes with grief
clutching her abdominal
walls   third time
this week …

I felt so powerless back then. I would just sit there or lay there beside her—exhausted—'til all hours of the night, watching her in so much pain. Talk about transferring anxiety. Maggie was a little sponge. That's how our divorce and my early recovery affected her. Poor baby.

… I ~~furtively~~   secretly sigh
while she nibbles ceremoniously
on the english muffin   I've slathered
with peanut butter   as she sheepishly
says   that's all she can eat…

Moving slow   she whimpers
into her jacket   bundled over   as
she pries open   the door.
Puddles form in my eyes   as
I watch her   through mud
splattered panes…

MAGGIE March 14

I got the stomach flu. Mom was up with me for two hours as I hunched over the toilet, retching my guts out, and then stayed with me while I was trying to get to sleep. She was at my beck and call. At one point I started thinking, oh god, how will I ever make it on my own? I'd never thrown up that much before. I hate puking. That was two days ago. Now she's just annoying me again.

CAROL Friday, March 16

Still no word from Amy Hsu. Will I ever get these darn Cows published?

MAGGIE March 16

I still haven't lived down the Harlem thing. I was the one who was directing the group on the subway. Oops. The aftermath of the trip, i.e. getting sick, gave me more proof to a theory I have: my failure to deal with the stress in my life leads me to getting sick. I overdo something, then I yak. Reason enough to not push myself too far. Can I learn to do that before I go to college?

Did I really say college? ACK!

chapter six

_____

Sex, Drugs, Rick 'n' Roll, and Seatbelts

CAROL Sunday, March 18, 10:33pm

Standing at the sink in my yellow rubber gloves, ready to dip those babies into a tub of dirty dishes, I heard a crashing sound out the window.

Kaboom. Squish. Shit. What the hell was that?

The carport had collapsed on my Geo Prizm. I just finished paying for the damn thing.

I went into a trance. Paced from the kitchen to the family room and back again. It wasn't until my neighbor knocked on my door that it became real. I fell into his arms and sobbed.

We stood outside, assessing the damage. It was hard to take in. The roof of my car was sitting in the back seat. I should've listened to Jason Russell from channel 40 weather. He told us to make sure to shovel off those roofs just last week. Damn.

I called the insurance company and left a message. I phoned my sister and friends for support. Pennie appeared lickety-split—to see if I was okay—to take me back to her house if I wanted to go. She offered me one of their cars as long as I needed. I opted for home—called my daughter at her dad's—to cushion the shock before seeing the rubble in the morning.

I thanked Pennie as much as I could for the car loan. Her kindness over-whelms me.

CAROL   Monday, March 19, sometime

I woke up so depressed, I could hardly move. Forced myself out of bed. It was hard to get dressed. My arms and legs were surely filled with the scrap metal from the car. Hadn't felt like this since Rickey left. I'm so tired of doing it all. I miss having back-up. Someone to take over when I feel paralyzed like this. Could it be I'm missing Rickey?

I had to call the insurance companies again. How would I ever make those calls, certain my arm could never lift that phone? Each task was a burden, until I popped opened my laptop and wrote about it. As words poured forth, I sensed it might work as a commentary.

MAGGIE   March 19

Mom called me at Dad's last night. You know that feeling you get in the pit of your stomach when you know something's wrong? I got that feeling when she called. I thought someone had died. Someone had. Our car. Totally squashed.

It's a good thing she called. Otherwise I would have freaked out if I just saw it getting off the bus. Broken glass all around, splinters of wood and all. And our poor car. It looked as though it had been in a rollover, several times.

CAROL   Tuesday, March 20

I finished the essay and emailed it to the news director at *WFCR*. He wants to run it Friday. I drove to Amherst for the taping. After the assessor deemed my car TOTALED.

CAROL   Thursday, March 22

Amy Hsu called. To say the publication committee rejected "The Day the Cows Got Loose." My god. She led me on for almost a year. All that time and energy—for what? No book contract, no money.

Five minutes later, the home owner's adjuster appeared at my door. "What do you want?" I growled. He stammered.

"Uh… I'm here to assess the damage." I wanted to bite his leg off.

By the time Maggie got home, I was shaking. Much to my surprise, her arms that almost never reach out to me anymore (sigh), wrapped themselves tightly around my torso, as the words," ah, Mom," slid gently from her mouth. It was the comfort I needed. The thing she did so easily just four years ago.

CAROL Friday, March 23

Turning on the radio at the foot of the stairs, I set the dial to *Morning Edition*. I settled on the bottom step, while Maggie sat on the top (I'd woken her early for this.) We waited, as the news surged through the speakers. Where was my commentary? Maggie looked annoyed.

Then Bob Paquette's smooth voice chimed in and introduced my piece. My toes tingled. And when I glanced up at Maggie, her chin resting on her hands, staring down at me as she listened, a smattering of pride spread across her face—a look I rarely see—and I knew all was right. That brief moment with my daughter on this Friday morning in March was worth it all.

MAGGIE March 23

Some good has come out of all this mess. Mom wrote a commentary and read it on NPR. It was wicked cool. Although she spoke way too slow, which made her sound funny. But still, very cool.

MAGGIE March 24

It's all Meyers's fault. I've lost my confidence as a writer. I can't even write this dumb paper about seeing *Rent*. Why can't I get what she wants?

CAROL Friday, March 30, 9:50pm

I met Len mid-week. I longed to be wrapped in his arms. He left his office at noon and took the Cross Sound Ferry from Orient Point to New London. I stopped on my way to buy him a rose. My heart was pounding as I watched the ferry pull into the slip. His face was clenched like a fist. As the afternoon wore on, he called his office way too many times. And rambled on about clients and colleagues. ugh.

We meet at the ferry on W~~ednesday~~
nesday my request for priority
satisfied with a midweek tryst...

> *...Hidden from ~~your~~ view*
I wait with red rose in hand
for you to appear...
> > *...a Wall*
Street warrior having shed
little of the financial strife
you should have left behind.

We'll never do that again. Maybe he doesn't care as much as I want him to.

MAGGIE April 4

I can't believe this. Louise just blurted out to me today that she slept w/Jerry over Christmas break. That was months ago! And she's only telling me now. Josh even knew about it before I did. She told me in chorus, and Josh was all "You didn't know that?" No, I didn't *know that*, asshole. Though I should have. One of my best friend's loses her virginity, and I don't hear about it until months after the fact. What the hell? How did I get so out of the loop? And why did Louise sleep w/Jerry? They weren't even dating then. This is all too crazy for me.

CAROL Thursday, April 5, 10:36pm

Greg sent a sample for the cover of "DIVORCE PAPERS." Oh my gosh. The color is divine. It's called Bordeaux Purple. I want to pore it into a goblet and sip on it. What are you talking about? You never sipped a glass of wine in your life!

I think of Joanie. How she helped me with this project. Read every poem over and over again.

Her car slips into the drive its engine purring to a halt. She steps out breathing in the forsythia that welcomes her. Standing at the door slender hands embracing manila folder I watch from my kitchen window as her eyes wander through the bouquet of spring. Letting her in 'How vulnerable do you feel?' sidles from her lips.   Sitting together   we haggle over words   combing through tresses of verse untangling snarls of prepositions   and shags of verbs   matted in poetry   that chronicled my divorce.   Sipping tea to soothe the ache   these poems produce   preparing myself once more to let go.   Satisfied with the grooming   I dig a spray of forsythia and slide it into a white sac   to grow like poesies in the garden of her soul.

MAGGIE   April 7

Mom, Ann and I went to see *The Vagina Monologues* tonight. I was hesitant about seeing something with the word 'vagina' with my mom, but it worked out okay. The word vagina is so taboo in our culture, more so than penis.

But these monologues were impressive! Some were serious, dealing with oppression and rape, while others were hilarious. There was one monologue which has been nicknamed "The Moaner." All Dar Williams did was utter different types of moans. It was great. We laughed so much.

After Ann's grandparents picked her up, Mom and I went out for pizza. We talked about how much we love Northampton. It's the best town, with awesome food, clothing stores, two great theaters that play Indies. Everything you could want. I'll miss it when I go to college. I don't even want to think about that now.

I'm still confused about marine biology. This bites.

CAROL   Saturday, April 7, 11:46pm

I was nervous about taking these teenagers to this show, not sure how it would be. I'm from the generation of women who once used 'down there' in reference to the female anatomy. I've forgotten how old I was when I first heard the word clitoris. My mother never used such terms or even spoke about sex. There I was—listening to all that taboo language with Maggie and Ann.

The performance made us proud to be women. Though, Maggie and Ann giggled through most of the stories.

If our vagina could talk, what would it say?
Slow down.
Feed me.
Yum, yum…

They howled.

If your vagina got dressed, what would it wear?
Red-high tops and a Mets cap worn backwards.

I cheered.

Maggie plans to write a paper about the show for her English class. Totally unimaginable to me at that age. Not something I would've plopped on a nun's desk first thing in the morning. I hope she asks me to copy edit for her. I snicker at the thought.

MAGGIE April 8

I'm doing research for my paper. Found out Eve Ensler (now known as V), spent two months in Croatia and Pakistan in 1994, interviewing Bosnia women refugees. And learned "20,000 to 70,000 women were being raped in the middle of Europe in 1993, as a systemic tactic of war...but over 500,000 women were being raped every year in this country," my god, "and in theory we were not at war." That's what the monologues were based on. Shit. It's not really safe being a woman. Do I really want to go away to college?

MAGGIE April 9

I don't think I ever realized what a sweet guy Dave is until today. At lunch, we somehow got talking about sex and Dave told me he wanted to wait until he found someone he loved. So sweet! Thank God my guy friends aren't stereotypical jerks who just want to get laid. I love my guys!

CAROL April 10, 11:20pm

I finished reading the last chapters of "Hillary Garfunkel" to my writer's group last night. And took a trunk-load of criticism about the novel. I flew out of there feeling angry and confused. Angry they came down on me so hard, confused about how to fix the damn thing.

Will I ever be a real writer? I would have liked a day of nothing but revising. Instead, I hobnobbed with insurance assessors and car sellers. I think I found the car I like.

When Mag got home, I was grossly pre-occupied with the number of calls

I still had to make. So I could firm up the car deal. I could tell she wanted my company. She had burned a CD of favorite female artists and longed for me to listen. I agreed, desperate for her approval and attention. I can't deal with her disappointment right now or with her being mad at me. After listening a while, I ordered Chinese take-out. Certain that sesame chicken would bring some balance back to my life.

MAGGIE   April 10

Ode to Chinese Takeout

Dew clings to white.
It shines in the light.
Peaks of orange reek of temptation.
Even to the fly.
Such a strong thing.
This little wire and cardboard.
Dinner is served.

MAGGIE   April 11

I'm re-reading *Animal Farm* for my final English paper. I forgot how much I love this book. The setup is perfect. Animals creating the perfect government for the farm, but it was eventually corrupted by the pigs. The fact that the pigs are corrupt is ideal. That was a nice touch by Orwell.

"All animals are equal, but some animals are more equal than others." That line completely sums up the corruption of Communism, or any society, for that matter. It morphed from a beautiful idea, "All animals are equal," to a power-hungry, uncontrollable basis for leadership. It's too bad I can't just write about this for my paper. Oh no, I have to be much more inventive than that. So, I'm also writing on *1984* and *Homage to Catalonia*. I think I'll write about the effect rumors had on the revolutions in such books. I hope Meyers finds it acceptable. I can't really think of anything else.

I think I've got my conclusion figured out, or at least part of it. "Orwell's novels are not only a lesson in what a government with absolute control can do, but the power of obscured tongue and thought can decide the future."

CAROL Wednesday, April 11, 10:38pm

I feel like I'm ready to send "The Day the Cows Got Loose" to a new crop of editors. Am I ever ready for more rejection? And will I ever get to be a real author?

I stopped and made copies anyway.

After dinner, Mag convinced me to hear more of her CD. "Please, Mom. These songs really rock." Before gathering in her room, I checked email, only to find a rejection from *Salon* for an essay I submitted. And geesh, I didn't divorce on Mother's Day, Amy!!

Dear Carol,

Thanks for thinking of us. I love the idea of you divorcing on Mother's Day, but I'm afraid this one doesn't quite work for us.

Best,

Amy

I'm over that edge I teeter on these days. I can't stand this anymore.

So, as Sarah McLaughlin's words curled around my ears, I sat on Maggie's bed, licking tears from both cheeks. When I need to break down, music will often get me to do it. I went to my room and cried 'til I was done.

We finished the night watching *Jesus Christ, Superstar,* on PBS. We sang along and discussed our views of Jesus—and what he's meant to the world. For me, he personifies love, compassion and forgiveness. I was raised Catholic, but left the church after college. Though I still embrace what Jesus embodied.

When they crucified Jesus, Maggie broke into tears. It was a touching moment for us. My dear Maggie, who rarely shows me her soft side anymore, expanded my heart with love. A meaningful end to a difficult day.

MAGGIE April 12

I hate Meyers. She's so demanding. Nothing's good enough for her. If I have to step into her class one more time, I'll puke. Or I might go into a psychotic rage and kill her. I'm leaning towards the second. Good thing vacation starts next week. Maybe now's the time to move to Canada. Especially if I'm on the run from the cops. I wonder if they have extradition laws...

CAROL Friday, April 13

These divorce poems have cracked me wide open, leaving me so vulnerable. All the old pain is leaking out. And this carport thing has really stressed me out. Shit. When will I stop crying?

This whole publishing process has been so frustrating. Makes me want to throw things. Anyway, I ended up sending the 'Cow's' manuscript to three more editors today. As Jane Yolen always says, "It won't be accepted if it's sitting on your desk." She also advises us not to multiply submit. Oh well.

I got another letter from Greg saying he won't be ready for a Mother's Day release of "DIVORCE PAPERS." Our latest in a long line of publication dates and delays. I hate this project right now.

MAGGIE April 13

Brien shocked the hell out of me today, and yet he didn't. On the bus ride home, he just blurted out, "Oh by the way, Waren came out." There has always been this voice inside my head that said he was gay. I just haven't seen him much since he moved to his dad's house. This explained a lot. Why he always had so much fun playing dress-up when we were little. Of course, that still doesn't explain Brien's willingness to dress-up too.

But I could smack Brien for being so blunt. Very smooth.

CAROL Saturday, April 14

We picked up my new car at Nicky D's. It rocks, as Maggie would say. Another Prizm, this time with a sunroof and CD player, bought to satisfy the teenager in me. Pennie held my hand through it all. She lent me money my insurance didn't cover. What would I do without her in my life? It also reminds me how I'm up to my friggin' eyeballs in debt.

She has been so generous with me. Sometimes it scares me. I worry about how this will affect our friendship. Will I start making decisions based on how much she gives me? Can I say no when I need to say no? What can I give her in return? I also question my worthiness. Oy. All this stinkin' thinkin' can get a gal down.

MAGGIE April 15

I'm haunted by Waren. How many people can say the first guy they kissed turned out to be gay? In some ways, it's pretty cool. I've got my own 'Will,' which every girl needs. I just hope I'm not as neurotic as Grace.

And yikes, I take my first college tour tomorrow!

CAROL Monday, April 16

I slept lousy last night. Nervous about our first college tour, especially at one of those $35,000/year places. Rickey will flip if she gets accepted. My heart was racing when I woke up. You'd think I was the one who was going to college.

We spent the day with Nat at Hampshire College in Amherst. After registration, we sat in on a class called Shakespeare and Wolfe. The professor didn't lecture, just worked on getting a discussion going on the reading material.

After that first class, we split up. Mag & Nat sat in on 'Sex, Drugs, Rock & Roll and Seatbelts' (surely named to draw more students) and I went to a women's studies course run by two professors, with only six students in the class. Great student/faculty ratio. I nearly dozed off. Couldn't get away with it in a class that size.

The girls had interviews before an informational meeting. Then we toured the campus. The dorms had tiny single rooms, with claustrophobically narrow hallways connecting them. What if there's a fire? Or she doesn't make any friends? What if she forgets to eat or stays up too late? Or skips too many classes? What if she gets date raped? Or meningitis? Or pregnant? Cripes. Will she even get in? How could we possibly afford to send her to Hampshire College? Will Rickey talk to me again if she goes here?

Shut down the mindless chatter or you'll freak out. I'm already there!

MAGGIE April 16

Hampshire College is a completely non-traditional kind of school. Very independent-based and I'm not sure I can handle it. Mom thinks I can, but I don't know. They don't give tests, so writing papers is the main form of evaluation. After my year in Meyers's class, I'm not sure my writing's good enough to handle that kind of assessment. Each day, I lean toward a more traditional college.

I think I just need to visit more schools. Hopefully, one with a regular theater. Hampshire only has black box. I did not like that black box theater. Too dark and enclosed.

MAGGIE April 17

We leave for Long Island tomorrow. To visit Southampton College. Known for its Marine Biology Dept. Is this really what I want to do? I hope I can sleep.

CAROL Saturday, April 21, 10:21pm

We just got back from Long Island. We stayed with Kathy in Water Mill. This was our first extended trip in the new car, and as usual, we fought over music on the way to the ferry. I get pulled into my teenage self when I'm with her. It's so annoying. So this new sun-roofed car, with CD player blasting, seems to suit us both.

When we got to Kathy's, Maggie slipped into a comfortable place with Liz, who's a year younger than Mag. They hung out—talking their teen talk—and laughed together throughout the visit.

The next day, we headed for the college. Mag was having doubts about the major. "Mom, I'm just not sure anymore." She made up her mind this visit.

We had time to spare before lunch with Len, so we cruised into Southampton and found a small museum exhibiting work by Carrie Mae Weems. Large scrims with her photographs printed on them hung from the ceiling, while music by Lionel Hampton drifted through speakers. Maggie was fascinated with her photos and immediately saw the connection between the art and music, while I mostly worried about our lunch with Len. What will they talk about? I hope she's civil to him! Jeez! What if she's rude? This was getting tiresome. Maybe even obsessive. Can't I be somebody else—besides me—for just one day?

The lunch actually went well. Maggie was pleasant and Len was charming, listening thoughtfully, supporting the college choices she's made. I was pleased with the way they got along.

That night, Kathy, Mag, Liz and I howled over stories Kathy and I told from our early 20s—when Lana, Ed, Antoinette, Merry, Kathy and I shared her childhood home—taken over by us when her parents moved to East Hampton. We laughed about the all-nighters we pulled playing bridge, monopoly or knock-hockey—and making chocolate chip cookies at the drop of a hat. Having to wait 17 seconds before we ate them. Ed's timing to obtain the very best taste was down to a science. We laughed about Ed's antics.

On Friday, Mag and I drove out to Montauk. We passed the bar where I met Dustin Hoffman. I described the night he sat behind Merry and I in a booth. When I tapped him on the shoulder and casually said, "I heard you wanted to meet me before I left." I sucked in my cheeks while he painstakingly tried to figure out who I was. And finally said, "You look so familiar. Where do I know you from?" I told him he might have seen me in the audience of one of his movies. What a hoot!

We drove to Ditch Plains, the campgrounds where we tented on weekends with Pat. Told Maggie about the nights we'd have gin & tonics with Truman Capote, with strings of Chinese lanterns dangling around his campsite. His trailer was a weekend retreat for hordes of his flamboyant friends.

Memories of that carefree time came flooding back. By the time we pulled into our driveway, I was exhausted—full of the love and remembrances we gathered on our trip.

MAGGIE April 21

I decided almost immediately I didn't want to go to Southampton. I liked the campus, but I realized I don't really want to do Marine Biology. Mom and I were sitting in a room with a bunch of other biology majors, and this guy was explaining what the biology department was like and what majoring in marine biology entailed. And while I was listening to him, I was struck with the realization that I had no interest in what he was saying. The idea of studying marine biology didn't excite me anymore. Mom and I left right after that. She had a hard time letting go of the marine biology thing. Poor Mom. She'll be a basket case when I leave for college. I'm the center of her life.

Lunch with Len went surprisingly well. I haven't seen him since I was seven, so this was a new experience for me. He reminds me a lot of Dad. They're both smart and funny, and sensitive and caring. But Dad's taller than Len.

They got into a fight. Len was surprised that Mom wasn't letting me look at colleges out west. Mom didn't like him butting in. She asked if he would let

Anna go to school in California. He said sure he would. Mom didn't believe him. But he was very supportive of me going, so he's in the plus category now. It would be cool to go to school in California. I doubt it will happen, but still....

So lunch was good, then Mom and I went out to Montauk the next day. She used to live there and she showed me all the places she used to hang out.

We stopped by Gurney's Inn. Mom and Merry worked as chambermaids there when they were young. They made Woody Allen's bed. And drank beers with some guy named Jimmy Breslin—right after he ran with a guy named Norman Mailer for mayor of New York. Mom said he had a room overlooking the ocean, where he sat at his typewriter and revised his novel, *World Without End, Amen*. She said he was kinda' crazy then, that his fingers were constantly combing through his hair.

We had a good time. Actually, the most fun was listening & singing along to the music in the car. We did lots of Beatles.

MAGGIE   April 23

I'm shocked how easy it was to let go of marine biology. It was my dream. Letting go of it was so easy. I think I might want to major in theater now.

MAGGIE   April 26

I'm really tired of going down to Dad's and eating by myself. That's what they do. They don't eat until late, so I'm left all by myself, hidden in the basement like I'm some kind of a leper or something.

CAROL   Friday, May 4, 9:46pm

Today I was the keynote speaker at a poetry event in the chapel of the Hampden County Correctional Center, for women graduating from their alcohol and drug rehab writing program. I helped them celebrate National Poetry Month. What an honor to be invited to this event!!

It reminded me of my days as clerk for the court bail program in Philly. I'll never forget the day I went to the men's unit at Holmesburg Prison to interview clients for release. I wore a baggy sweater to hide my body. Talk about getting strip searched with the eyes. Skeevy guys leering out their cells with their eyes popping out. Kinda scary. That place was a throw back to the middle ages. Reeked of mold and sweat. Known for the medical experiments performed on inmates in exchange for pocket money. *Cripes.* That was actually going on when I was there.

MAGGIE   May 4

I'm scared I won't do well in theater. I also don't want to spend my life living paycheck to paycheck like Mom. She's always worried about money and uses her credit card way too much. I just know I don't want to live that way. And I have the feeling that's what would happen. But I love theater. What should I do? This stuff is so confusing.

CAROL   Saturday, May 5, 9:46pm

Maggie took another round of SATs. Saturday is our day to sleep in and do nothing. With all the pushing I've done the past 2 months, I needed a weekend void of anything besides watching videos and catching up on reading. Instead, I felt compelled to ignore my need for rest. I hate when I do that.

After the test, we had lunch at Teapot, a new Japanese place in Noho. Since we won't be together on Mom's Day—I'm off to a wedding next weekend, and Maggie goes to her junior prom—this felt right.

Being tired, I struggled to make conversation. She took advantage of my fatigue, looking for things to pick on, knowing I was vulnerable. I recognize the pattern—something I've done myself. She needs me to be strong now and gets mad when I'm not. But doing this college stuff with her, shoot, I'm missing her already.

Last night, she went to a party with her friend, Ann, while I caught a showing of *The Widow of St. Pierre*. I returned to fetch them at 10:30 or so. The moon was full. I opened the sun roof. The girls stood on the seats, soaking up the glorious spring air and light from the moon. They giggled like five-year-olds, dousing my heart with glee.

MAGGIE May 5

Took SATs this morning. That was fun, wait, no!

Ann and I went to a party at Jack's tonight. He really lives in the middle of nowhere. All woods. It was big fun though. Jack got Ethan to spin for us. He made this mix of Nine Inch Nail's "Closer" and the Spice Girl's "Wannabe." Very weird, but it works. As long as you hate the Spice Girls. And everyone took turns playing pool. Joe was so determined to beat Connie, he resorted to cheating. By cursing the cue ball and humping Connie's back while she took her shots. He did all this while wearing fishing waders. It was a beautiful moment.

Mom picked us up way too early. But on the drive home, Mom opened the moon roof, and Ann and I jumped up on seats to hang out of the car. I felt like I was Tom Hanks in *Big*. The only thing missing was ice cream.

CAROL Sunday, May 6, 9:46pm

Ann spent the night and left early this morning. Mag and I were cranky and needy most of the day. Neither of us had much to give. On days like this, the slightest look of disapproval leads to fighting. And no matter how hard I try to change the dynamics, nothing seems to work. Both of us felt frustrated and unloved.

At some point, I got clear about what was happening and mentioned it to Maggie, which always seems to soften the edge between us. We've made a deal to never go to bed mad at each other. We were able to say goodnight in a somewhat civil and loving manner. Sometimes that's all I can hope for.

MAGGIE May 6

Something I've recently realized is I let Mom take all the blame for our problems. I manipulate her feelings of guilt to let myself off the hook. I may not be able to change that in the heat of the moment, but later on, I need to suck it up and look at my part in the problem.

CAROL Monday, May 7

Shit. Got stopped today for rolling through a friggin' stop sign. Then had my new car towed for an expired registration. How can the registration be expired? I just got the damn thing three weeks ago!! The officer who stopped me had a new recruit with him. I think he was out to impress him. I was so angry all I could do was cry. And pay the $90 they charged for towing my car away. I owe $100 for an expired registration. It's exhausting being me.

MAGGIE May 7

Woot! I got my invitation to Academic Society in homeroom today. Ann, Natasha, Louise, Jeanne, Dave, Carrie, Dingle and Kailey all got in too. This is so awesome. If only for the fact that once I'm inducted, I won't need a pass to go out into the halls anymore. Which will make senior year much more enjoyable. And it's going to be important for my college application.

MAGGIE May 8

Ted unveiled the set for *Midsummer* today at drama. It is *so* cool. It's a set of wooden platforms, all at different levels and heights. It spreads across the whole stage and is covered in fake ivy and flowers. But it does offer lots of opportunities for slivers in my feet, so I have to watch out for that. We fairies also got our costumes. They're pillowcases. Or at least, they're pillowcases with sleeves and scalloped hems. Seriously. They only hit mid-thigh. Mine is mustard yellow. Oh, this is going to work out well. Let's see. A bunch of teenage girls crawling around stage wearing pillowcases. No one better be wearing thongs!

CAROL Thursday, May 10, 11:25pm

I'm gonna miss Maggie's prom. Breaks my heart. I have to find a way to move on with my life apart from hers. But still, I'm missing her prom! Hope Rickey takes tons of pictures.

CAROL Sunday, May 13, 9:15pm

I'm back from a weekend in New Jersey. My cousin's kids are getting married now. Makes me feel old. I went to Ma's on Friday and drove her to Cherry Hill for Danielle's wedding. We listened to a Platter's CD and held hands on the drive, singing along to some of the songs from Ma's time. It was so precious to me. Times like this seem so rare. Our relationship has been almost as turbulent as the one she had with Dad. My eyes sting as I write this.

Of course, Len was there (we share the same family—his father is a twin brother to my uncle—so his cousins are my cousins too). It was the first time we were together as a couple with the rest of the family. A big stretch for Len. He's such a private person. We danced and laughed, and shared a room. I love who I am with him—totally myself. More than with anyone.

I find it so hard to say goodbye to him. This time it was compounded by other family being there. Our farewells go on forever, as did my tears. I'm so open-hearted these days.

Plus, I got to spend Mother's Day weekend with Ma!

MAGGIE May 25

The play went well. I only had one stanza of lines, so it wasn't a very stressful production. Leigh and Cassie's fight scene was incredible. This big cat fight. I mean, what else could it be with the line "to scratch out her eyes"? Only thing that went wrong was the splinter I got in my hand. I knew it would happen sooner or later. But I just love theater. I think I should major in it.

CAROL Friday, May 25

Sui and Phil came down to see Maggie in *A Midsummer Night's Dream*. I love that they do this. We feel so supported by them. Mag & I had a little cake for Sui's birthday, which I brought up to school with me. We stuck a candle on it and sang happy birthday in the parking lot before they headed back to Vermont.

MAGGIE May 26

I just found out I have to audition at BU to be accepted into their theater program. Apparently the theater department is a conservatory. I've never auditioned. And my first time is going to be for college!! This is not good. Do I really want to major in theater?

CAROL Wednesday, May 30, 10:20pm

Kevin Lewis, the Senior Editor from Simon & Schuster Books for Young Readers, called about "The Day the Cows Got Loose." He likes it. He really, really likes it. He also wants to see a copy of "IT'S NOT FAIR." YES!! Wait'll I tell Leslie!

Of course, he still has to take it to the dreaded publication committee. All the people who would work with the book. The marketing people have a big say in the acceptance process. I've heard they're hard to impress. What if they don't like it as much as Kevin does? Please let them fall in love with it... pretty please.

MAGGIE May 31

Oh god. This is so terrible. Today at school we were told Mrs. Warren has liver cancer. So that's why she's been out sick. I'm having these horrible flashbacks to sixth grade, when Mrs. Chevrette died. From a cerebral hemorrhage. Everyone in class started to cry. And I hadn't even had her as my teacher. God, I hope Mrs. Warren doesn't die. I mean, how many teachers/truckers/quilters do we have in the world?

CAROL Friday, June 1

I sent Kevin a copy of "IT'S NOT FAIR" as he asked. I also heard from one of the inmates I met after I gave my keynote address at the correctional center earlier this month. She sent me some of her poems. Her words transform such a scary situation into works of art. Of course, I wrote back and praised her brave and powerful writing.

MAGGIE June 4

Must focus. I have to finish this paper. It's my last one. I can see the light at the end of the tunnel. I just hope it's not a train.

CAROL Tuesday, June 5, 11:40pm

The first copy of "DIVORCE PAPERS" is completely printed, gathered and folded. Yay! Greg found some errors while binding it. Shoot. He said he can fix the mistakes, but that will slow up production. It's always something….

MAGGIE June 8

I went to senior graduation. It kind of sucked going by myself, but I wanted to say goodbye to the people graduating a year above me. Specifically, Leigh, Claire, Amy, Mallory and Cassie. It's going to be weird without them next year. I still have Leigh and Mallory's grad parties to go to, which means more of the same goodbyes. Fun. More crying.

Of course, I'm having a bit of a nutty night, 'cause it's going to be me up there next year. ACK! I'm a senior now!!

Untitled (2)

The sickness in my stomach
tells me to run far away.
Reflections in the mirror
are my future.
Let someone else
go first.
Slam the door,
walk to my doom.
Where did that
noise come from?
This isn't the real deal.

MAGGIE June 13

I can't believe it. I actually got a B on my last paper for Meyers. YEA!! Maybe I should major in English.

MAGGIE June 14

Oh god. It's 3:00 am. I can't sleep. I can't stop thinking about Kingsley's trig class. I can't go in tomorrow. If I get a D, I'm screwed.

CAROL Friday, June 15, 11:00pm

Today started poorly. Tried every trick I knew to get that girl out of bed, short of pulling the covers off. (I'm not that bad after all.) Forbidding her to attend Mallory's party didn't help—not being reasonable or related—those kinds of consequences don't work anymore. So, after marching back to her room seven or eight times, trying desperately to pry her out of bed, I finally caved in (or gave up). I'm not totally sure which is more accurate.

The truth is, I felt having her home would be intolerable. What kind of mother says that?

I reluctantly picked up the receiver, happy when an unrecognizable voice answered the phone. The last time she stayed home, I promised it would be my last call to her school. There I was, breaking the promise I'd made to myself.

Morning is not my strong time of day. I often feel like I'm ten when I wake up. Maggie takes advantage of any weakness she sees in me.

So after I called school, I went back to bed. Then stayed in my jammies the rest of the day. By the time Mag got up at 2:00, I succumbed to watching movies with my truant teen, *Good Will Hunting* and *A Clear and Present Danger,* were our picks of the day.

I reminded Mag of her dish duty. As always, she gave me backlash. It makes me furious, resorting to tactics only siblings would contrive. I took the phone off the hook so she couldn't get online. She returned to the scene and shouted her case—pulling me into a power struggle I gladly oblige to these days. An hour later, I grew weary of the game, distressed by the mentality initiating it, and hung up the phone.

I'm so anxious about this book deal with Simon & Schuster, I couldn't help myself. It was really pathetic.

MAGGIE June 17

Only a few more days left of school. I skipped on Friday, which started off a doozy weekend. Friday was D-day in Kingsley's trig class, meaning you find out whether or not you have a D in 4th quarter. Unfortunately, he doesn't allow people to have D's in 4th quarter, so it goes down to an F. The last time I checked, I had a D. I was terrified to find out my grade, which caused me to be sick Friday morning. Mom just thought I wanted to skip so I wouldn't have to get up, but it wasn't that. The idea of failing kept me up the night before, and the night after that, and last night. I've never failed a class before. And I know your grades aren't a reflection of you and all that crap, but an F sure seems like a reflection of me. A reflection of my suckiness.

CAROL Monday, June 18, 8:49pm

It started as a simple attempt to mow knee high grass surrounding the house. I do let go of some things. I tripped over the back steps with the gas can in my hand, toppling onto the concrete slab surrounding the back porch. Needing comfort and first aid, I stumbled up stairs and down the hall to Maggie's room, heaving from tears, where she willingly came to my rescue.

She grabbed my hand and led me down the hall to the bathroom—as tears cascaded down my cheeks. That's when Nurse Maggie kicked in. Pouring hydrogen peroxide over the cuts, she gently blew on them, easing the sting, and bandaged me up like a first rate practitioner. I prattled about my inner wuss, bursting us into fits of laughter. Since I long for those kinds of moments with her, this quite possibly was not an accident. Evidently, I need a long vacation or a three hour session with my therapist.

MAGGIE June 18

It's a surreal feeling to be the protector, so to speak. I don't like seeing my mommy hurt. OK, enough with the baby talk.

chapter seven

_____

Can't Stop Sobbing

CAROL Thursday, June 21

I could see the tears well up in Maggie's eyes as her lips quivered. I grabbed her hand and held on tight. It felt so surreal. I tried to grasp the words that floated from Dr. Alder's mouth—I heard what she said—thought I knew what they meant—but fought to misinterpret them 'cause I didn't want it to be true.

A mass under her tongue?

Needing to schedule another appointment, I slumped at the reception desk in the waiting room from hell, while Maggie fled to the car. By the time I got outside, she was leaning against the Prizm, drenched from pouring rain, arms wrapped tightly around her chest and sobbing. She cried the rest of the way home, not saying a word.

As we drove along, I told her to cry as much as she needed, to let it all out. I dug down and felt a strength I forgot I possessed. I made a decision I wouldn't go to that panic place I always go to—that I would stay in the moment and not jump ahead to what might be. I decided not to worry needlessly. Maggie needed me to stay strong.

She needed me close all night. After she studied for her trig final, I helped her with her history notes. Like old times.

MAGGIE June 21

I was soaking wet. I couldn't get in the car and couldn't stop sobbing. Oh God. I probably have cancer.

CAROL Friday, June 22

My mouth got dry and hands grew slippery on the wheel after dropping Maggie at her school for a class trip to a Red Sox game. Her dad would pick her up at 2:00am. As I drove home, the fear I was holding at bay, frantically tried to unleash itself. I keep a liberal stash of chocolate for times like this. My substitute for drinking.

Helps push down the fear I don't want to feel.

MAGGIE June 23

I didn't fail trig!! Don't know how that happened, I was just relieved that it did. As it turned out, Mr. Kingsley, this man who I thought was one of the hardest teachers at HRHS, has ended up being one of my favorites. I've learned more in his class than any other math course I've had. That seems to be my pattern with school: a difficult teacher I hate during the year ends up being the best.

Saying that about Kingsley is a lot easier than saying it about Meyers though. I can't imagine ever admitting it to her face.

One good thing about obsessing over my trig grade is, it kept me from obsessing about the thing under my tongue. Thank goodness for the Red Sox game, which was a major distraction. Except they lost. Now I've got nothing to distract me from it. I just don't want to think about it. I can't think about it. 'Cause if I do, I'll freak out and won't be able to deal with the next few days. So, no more thoughts about cancer or death.

CAROL Monday, June 25

We can't see the oral surgeon for another 2 weeks. How will we ever make it till then?

MAGGIE   June 26

I spent the last week in total fear. Couldn't even talk to my friends about it. It would make it real.

CAROL   Thursday, June 28

I got a letter from Margery Cuyler today. She's an editor at Winslow Press. She likes "The Day the Cows Got Loose." Yikes. Now what do I do? Hold her off while Kevin sells the 'Cows' to the pub committee? This is exactly what Jane Yolen warned us about. Only send to one editor at a time, because if you should be so lucky to have more than one interested, you're in a fix. I guess I'm lucky *and* in a fix. Helps take my mind off Maggie.

MAGGIE   June 28

What?
Feel sick I.
   Is strange which.
      That I feel sick not.
         Always sick I'm.
            Why I feel sick but.
               Should be happy I.
                  For joy jumping.
                     I feel sick but.

I can't do this. I think I'll just get it over with and stick my head in the oven. Oh shit. It's electric.

CAROL   Sunday, July 1, 11:38pm

We've been having trouble with our water this week and today the pressure was really low. I should own stock in the frigging duck tape business from all the home repair work I've done with it.

Oh god. What if she has cancer?

Our cellar is more like a dungeon this time of year—cold and wet—with clusters of spider webs adorning the ceilings and walls. Taking the lid off the pressure switch, I noticed a carbon stain. Something was burning out, along with a deteriorated connection in the pressure switch itself. Cripes, I could take the place of 'what's his name' on *Home Improvement.*

This meant a trip to Home Depot. And since I'd promised Maggie a driving lesson today, we combined the events. Neal installed the new switch for me. And the bloody thing still doesn't work. This really can't be happening right now.

MAGGIE   July 1

Mom gave me a driving lesson today. It didn't go well. The car stalled in front of this huge tractor trailer that looked like it was ready to pounce on us at the intersection. Mom and I changed seats and looked like some film clip from the keystone cops. From now on, maybe I should take lessons from Dad! If I'm lucky enough to live that long. Oh god.

CAROL   Friday, July 6, 10:20pm

We spent the 4th in Woodstock, at Sui's home in Vermont, playing croquette to the wee hours of the morning. A much needed distraction for us. Good to be with Sui. She's always a comfort to us. Says Maggie will be fine.

We did our traditional cake walk. Sui made the big old cake we coat with whipped cream and decorate with blueberries and strawberries to look like the flag. Then we march around the house and yard, with silly hats on, holding the cake, and singing "You're a Grand Old Flag" and "Yankee Doodle Dandy." All those George M. Cohan songs from Ma's time. This year Judy wore a babushka and shawl, to illustrate the immigrant aspect of our history. We thought we'd die laughing.

When I wasn't smacking croquette balls or parading around with cakes, I thought about Maggie and the water pressure, wondering if I'd be pumping from the old porch well when we got home, and if she'd be okay.

MAGGIE July 6

We took a hike up Mt. Thom. Aunt Susie, Bobby, Meredith, Phil, Mom and I walked on the rocky side of the mountain on the way back down. We had to wait to get picked up by Uncle Phil and Judy. Mom had some cherries and we started eating them and spitting out the pits. Originally it was just to get some liquid out of them, 'cause we totally blanked on bringing water, but it turned into a huge contest. We laughed so much, Aunt Susie peed in her pants. Again!

As we laid watching the sky explode with Fireworks, I thought they looked more beautiful than ever before and wondered if these would be the last I'd see.

CAROL Sunday, July 8

Just thinking about when Mag was little—sigh—pushing her on the old tire swing that still hangs from the cherry tree out back. She loved it when I'd go under that thing so she could fly high. She wanted to touch the clouds and the sky. Please let my baby be all right.

I returned the faulty switch to Home Depot, now facing little or no water pressure, determined to fix it myself. After making three futile trips to the Westhampton General Store, I called Chris Campbell. Seems the water pump burned out, and my home owners insurance covered it. Hallelujah! While Chris was at it, he also added a new pressure switch that worked.

Reminds me of "Repairman" that Greg will use for "DIVORCE PAPERS." Must be feeling lonely. I'm missing Len. Need his arms around me. He's busy with his kids.

He puffs
on my back
stoop...

... says
it's his last
week him and the
wife are quitting
on Sunday.

...getting on each
other's nerves
fighting
walking away.

remembering
how it was
my loneliness
yearns for
one more
fight.

By the time Maggie got home, I was elated by my good fortune. She hadn't a clue what I'd gone through and didn't seem to care. Thank goodness we see the oral surgeon this week.

CAROL Monday, July 9

Still no word from Kevin Lewis. What's taking them so long?

MAGGIE July 10

We saw the oral surgeon. He was so sweet, and without a doubt, a hottie. All I care is that I have more than six months to live. No cancer.

CAROL Tuesday, July 10

Thank you, Goddess.

MAGGIE July 11

Mel told me that Chris has a crush on me. I already knew this. It's been pretty obvious for a while now. The term 'puppy dog' comes to mind. I'm not sure what to think. I know I have zero romantic interest in him. I guess the best strategy is to ignore it. Until Chris brings it up. Then I'll be dealing w/a whole new issue.

CAROL Thursday, July 12, 11:25pm

This week's dedicated to manuscript repair. Remodeled "Susie Skates," renovated "Limerick Lil," reworked "Will This Be the Year They Get Me," and revamped "Has Anyone Seen Santa" and "Everything Will Be Just Fine." One for each day of the week. Revising is fun after I haven't worked on a manuscript in a while.

I had some email contact with Rickey, quibbling back and forth about sending Maggie to college. He's so focused on the finances. It's aggravating. Maybe it's a guy thing. Which only makes it all the more irritating. It feeds my shame and guilt. The guilt I feel about being a writer and shame because I'm still getting money from him. Knock it off, Carol.

CAROL Friday, July 13

The suspense of waiting to hear from Kevin about the final acceptance of the *Cows* has turned me into an anxious freak. I really HATE when that happens. To add to this neurotic mix, I'm stuffing it down with sweets. Chocolate has become a major food group.

Needing a break from myself, I took Maggie to a baseball game around the corner from Rickey's. Mag was excited about seeing Bjorn play. It was a perfect day for baseball—with all the promise for an exciting game.

We fought half the way home. Battled over when we'd shop for a present Mag needed for a party the following night. I voted for now, when we were out, while Maggie preferred to wait, somewhere closer to the last minute. She wore me down and won.

She's more powerful these days. *The Pause* has diminished my mom-power. Though I did some negotiating (she calls it bribery) to get her help with some household chores. "If I agree to take you tomorrow, you have to help me make dinner tonight." She agreed. We grilled hamburgers and steamed some corn.

Bottom line—we had a good time at the game, which means loads to me right now.

MAGGIE July 18

I'm going to Hamilton with Dad and Teresa this weekend to visit Arlene. Thank God, 'cause Mom is driving me crazy. I desperately need to get out of this house. I feel claustrophobic. Is it Friday yet?

CAROL Friday, July 20, 11:59pm

I have this sense I'm starring in a dream. But while I was waiting to hear back from Kevin Lewis, I was stage-managing a nightmare. Knee-deep in anxiety. Nails bitten beyond the quick. Constantly on edge. Ready to jump down whoever's throat was there. Poor Mag! By the time Rickey picked her up today, I was in bad shape.

Then, at 4:30, the phone rang. I heard Kevin's melodious voice on my answering machine and knew this was it. "The Day the Cows Got Loose" is being published by Simon & Schuster. He said it was the 'most talked about book' at the meeting. Yowzer!! I've waited years for this.

It took a couple hours for it all to sink in. By then, I'd made lots of heart thumping calls. I tried to get Maggie at Arlene's [Teresa's mom], where she's spending the weekend with Rickey and Teresa. They hadn't arrived, but I passed on my news. She told Maggie the moment they walked through the door. Oh to have been a fly on the wall.

Mag called a few hours ago, beside herself with excitement. I think she'd given up on my ever getting any of my children's books published. I started submitting those manuscripts when she was eight. Bless her heart. We both agreed it was a great lesson in perseverance paying off.

MAGGIE July 20

There is nothing better at the end of a long trip, than having a grandmother offering baked goods and soup. I love Arlene. A stereotypical Grandma. One who packs you full of food as soon as you arrive. She spoils us so. I love it.

MAGGIE July 24

They like Mom's book. I'm really proud of her. I think she wrote it 10 years ago.

She's been writing for a long time. I'd given up hope she'd ever get anything published. I supported her for so long, I just got tired of having my hopes smashed along with hers. I'm really glad I was wrong.

CAROL Thursday, July 26

I wrote back to Margery Cuyler at Winslow Press. Told her I've accepted another publisher's offer. I revised the letter at least ten times. It's draining to have such little confidence in myself.

MAGGIE July 29

I am scum. No. I'm lower than scum. Actually, I take that back. Mel's lower than scum. I may have manipulated a friend last night, but it was Mel who forced me to do it.

We were all over Nat's and Chris's to film a big movie. Chris had written this wicked long script with a bunch of characters in it. It was a big deal to him. But as usual, everyone was goofing off. Chris got so pissed, he stormed off and refused to film anymore. And Mel, the good friend that she is, devised the perfect plan to get him back.

She convinced me to use Chris's feelings for me to get him to start filming again. The plan was for me to pout and beg Chris, then give him a big hug. So, Chris cops a feel and gets back to work. Hence, I am scum.

CAROL Wednesday, August 1, 10:55pm

I took Maggie and Ma to Seaside Heights, the place that capped off all our summer vacations as kids. We strolled around the amusement pier, holding onto Ma's hand, munching on fried dough. I cherish her Chaplin-esque toddle, taking in sights as we ambled along, delighting in our rejuvenated love.

The two of us watched my daredevil daughter brazen rides that made us gulp with fear. I succumbed to a whirl on the Wild Mouse, once considered the scariest ride on the boardwalk, back in the days it sat at the far end of the pier, with hair pin turns that hung over the deep black sea. Our time with Ma was delish.

MAGGIE August 3

We just got back from visiting Ma in New Jersey. Seeing her is always bitter-sweet, because I haven't had the best relationship with her. We've never been very close. Due largely in part to Mom's relationship with her when I was growing up. Mom was sorta at odds with her, and I took her lead from that. I never tried to please her, or make her love me, and I think she resents that. Mom says Ma is used to people trying to please her. But that's just not the type of thing I do. It's not like she was ever overtly mean to me or anything. Just little things. Like the time I freaked out driving over this giant bridge to Lavallette. She was all, "Why would you be scared about that?" Then she immediately jumped into a conversation about Andrew, who is definitely her favorite grandchild. Andrew has no problem pleasing Ma. But besides that, this trip was good.

The best part was taking Ma to Seaside Heights. There were tons of seagulls on the boardwalk and they kept dive bombing us. Not good. I hate seagulls. But I think Ma had fun. We ate funnel cake and got sugar all over us. And there were no fights, which was nice.

CAROL Wednesday, August 8

I went to the Cape to spend a few days with Joanie. Stopped by to see Aunt El and Uncle Chet on the way. Aunt El isn't doing well. She's had pneumonia a couple times this year. I'm worried about her. I know she misses Carl, and I pray her health returns. She's like a mom to me.

CAROL Thursday, August 9

Got a post card from Margery Cuyler saying, "CONGRATULATIONS on having placed The Day the Cows Got Loose. I know it's going to be a really delightful picture book."

How sweet! I'd love to work with her someday. I've heard so many good things about her from Jane Yolen. Maybe I should thank her for her note to me. I'll wait a little before I send another manuscript and thank her then.

MAGGIE August 10

Mom asked Ma to help us pay for my braces. Ma always wanted braces on her teeth, but her mother wouldn't let her get them. This is her way of making up for that. She still has all her own teeth. And she's 83.

CAROL Sunday, August 12

At dinner, Mag mentioned she asked Rickey if she could use his car for a party on Friday, gulp, as I gobbled down pork chops like some malnourished pig. "Aren't we rushing things?" I said with a snort. "You haven't even gotten your license yet!"

Later, we settled on a game of scrabble, that mysterious mix of letters and squares, easing the dread we both tasted tonight.

I sit here wondering who will reassure me, when images of Maggie flash in my mind, blasting the stereo as she bounces behind the wheel of Rickey's Cherokee, heading out to a party on her first solo spin? This could get very ugly. I don't think I'm ready for this.

CAROL Monday, August 13, 11:03pm

Tomorrow morning I take Maggie for her driving test. I fear she'll do fine. To-night we had a spat. Imagine that? She said, "Dad's still mad at you for buying a car with a manual transmission." Making his car the only one she can drive.

"Oh well. Too bad," I said. No tears shed this night.

But I think Maggie's mad too. She doesn't like driving my stick shift and is pissed I didn't get a car she can, a-hem, take over. I may be menopausal, but I'm no dummy.

MAGGIE August 13

My license test is tomorrow. ACK! I am *so* nervous. I really don't want to fail. But I think I'll be fine. Charlie, one of my instructors, said I'm an excellent driv-er, so that boosts my confidence some.

CAROL Tuesday, August 14

Driving to the registry
it's hard to say   who's
more nervous   she ~~or~~
or me.   After a year
of practice   she's taking
her driving test   and
I don't think   I've
rehearsed at all.   I don't
know how to   calm
myself   when I
I think of her
~~at~~ behind
the wheel
alone.

It's official. Maggie got her license.

MAGGIE August 14

No more depending on my parents for rides. Now I can take off on my own. Freedom baby. All I need is my own car. A black Porsche would be sweet.

CAROL Wednesday, August 15

I went to a hearing for the damn ticket I got in May. Thankfully, they waived the fine for the expired registration. But the roll-through…can't blame anyone but me. I hate that!

CAROL Thursday, August 16

I am beside myself. Airborne Express delivered a large manila envelope containing the offer letter from Simon & Schuster for "The Day the Cows Got Loose." This makes it official! Yowza!

CAROL Monday, August 20

We went to Skidmore College. I drove like a maniac to get us there on time. We liked the campus, but Maggie's not sure if the school is right for her. She has her heart set on BC.

MAGGIE August 20

Skidmore was okay. Mom thinks it's too far away. Shit. California is far away. Dad keeps pushing UMass. No way I'm going there. Too close to home.

But Tanglewood was good. Aunt Susie and Uncle Phil are the best. They brought a picnic and a cake to celebrate my birthday.

CAROL Friday, August 24, 11:47pm

We just got back from Boston. Went to visit Boston College. We fell in love with the campus. Some of the old buildings were breathtaking. Dorms were a bit cramped.

I remember when I came with friends for a Seton Hall/BC basketball game. How we crawled out the window of an apartment being raided by police. Joan Chisholm could always sniff out the wild parties.

Mag and I went to a Red Sox game with Lauren and Joe. They have held our hands on this college quest. We've been grateful for their support. Lauren took us to see BU this morning. The thought of Maggie in college in a big city has me worried. Seeing the campus helped to ease some fear.

MAGGIE August 24

BC and BU rock. I really hope I get into BC, but BU would be okay. Having Lauren and Joe close by would be good. I'm a little worried about it being a Catholic school, but the guy who gave us the tour of the campus said there is a large non-Catholic population, so I guess it's not that big a deal. The campus is beautiful. Perfect combination of old and new. And it's only a T ride into Boston. Just wish Dad would stop nagging me about UMass. I want to get away from here.

CAROL Saturday, August 25

If I have one more frigging hot flash tonight, I will tear someone's adenoids from their throat and rip them to shreds. I need sleep. Mag's friends are coming tomorrow for an early birthday party.

MAGGIE August 27

Ann, Marie, Beth and I piled into Marie's car and went to the Class Breakfast at East Mountain Country Club. We were all wasted from my birthday party. Most of us only got about two hours of sleep. Some none. This mealtime tradition officially makes us seniors. The food was awful, and all we did was mill around and talk for an hour or so. Dave made fun of how I take my coffee. I just don't understand how anyone can drink coffee w/o putting at least three sugars in it. At least he was sweet enough to give me a ride home. I just love Fuzzy Bunny. And I know he's waiting for the day I let that go. Never gonna happen, Dave! You're stuck w/that name forever.

CAROL Wednesday, August 29

School starts again next week. Maggie's last year at Hampshire Regional High School. I don't even want to think about it.

MAGGIE August 30

Mom and I got invited to Aidan and Diadra's wedding, on October 20th in Maryland. Mom said if we go, we should go to Washington, DC while we're down there. She hasn't made up her mind. Says it'll cost too much. Always says that.

CAROL Friday, August 31

I snuck into Maggie's room this morning and laid out the sonogram they took the day before she was born. When they told me I'd have to have a C-section. I remember crying all day. All those Lamaze lessons down the tubes. She was breech, her head butted into my ribs. Sometimes I think I can still feel the bruise.

I set all her congratulations baby cards around her bed. Saved them all. I laid out her first bib, her first booties, and her treasured binky. I get all sniffly. It's what I do every year. It's the birthday ritual for Margaret Louise Henley.

CAROL Monday, September 3, 11:10pm

Spent a wonderful weekend with Len. Took him to my favorite retreat.

After laying in bed for hours
catching up on months of unspoken ~~unspoken~~
spoken body language   we
mount bikes on racks and
head for the reservoir.
As we peddle around ~~the~~
the glistening pool   loons
dive for lunch   while ~~the~~ breeze
dissolves sweat from brows
and turns loosestrife into purple
bliss.   Melancholy sets in   as we
rest at ~~the~~ water's edge   dangling feet
over lapping ripples   breathing
in the benevolence of the
day   filling our senses
with apparitions
from the past.

I've decided to go to his nephew's wedding in October. Len says he'll bring his kids. We talked about meeting in D.C. and seeing the Vietnam Vet's Memorial. Maggie's so happy we're going. And that Anna and Luke will be with Len. Our first outing together with all our kids. Oy. Do I really want to do this? Traveling is stressful enough without adding this extra pressure to the mix. Besides, I really like having Len to myself.

MAGGIE September 4

I told Mom about the drinking thing today. Right there in Burger King. I couldn't keep it from her anymore. It's kind of annoying, not being able to keep any big secrets from my mother. I'm not sure I like she has that kind of power over me.

I told her I had a sip of what I thought was an alcohol-free drink, and that I watched some of my friends drink more later that night. It really bothered me. They've never shown any interest in alcohol before. It's one of the reasons I like hanging out with them. I was really upset. But after talking to Beth, who was also bothered by it, I decided to accept the fact and go from there. They're my friends, and I love them. But if they start to drink, Beth and I will just hang out together.

Mom made me promise I wouldn't drive with anyone who's drinking. I'm resigned to being the designated driver or key master for my friends.

CAROL Tuesday, September 4, 11:10pm

School starts on Wednesday. Needing supplies, Mag and I pit-stopped for a brisk bite, where Mag provided details about information I'd already gotten from Donna—reporting that kids were drinking at some of their parties. "Drinking? Who's drinking? Are you drinking? You're not drinking, are you?" She's 17. Who am I kidding? Our family history of alcoholism urges me to freak out.

MAGGIE September 5

I'm a senior. Oh my god. Is this *really* my last year in high school? It seems so unreal. I'm still waiting for it to sink in.

CAROL September 6

Heard from Greg about "DIVORCE PAPERS." He said, "I'm pleased to report the printing is about 2/3rds done. Very pleased with how the sheets are going through the press…." I guess this thing is really gonna happen.

CAROL Thursday, September 9

I'm starting to freak out about college expenses. We are way over our heads. Maybe UMass *is* a good idea. It's not where Maggie wants to go. She wants to get away from here. Nancy recommended a consultant named Chris Illuzi. I'll have to call him. Soon…

MAGGIE September 10

It feels so great to be back in one of Mr. Mercus' English classes. Back with the teacher who gave me the highest mark on my final in ninth grade. 101 baby! I just love that Mercus doesn't stick to a syllabus. We go off on these random tangents in class, and I end up learning more than I ever have in any class before. Not just about grammar or literature, but politics, history, and culture. And it doesn't hurt that Mercus is a psycho Beatles fan. A man after my own heart.

CAROL Tuesday, September 11, 2001

I sent Maggie off to school and went back to bed. Still tired from a fitful night's sleep. I drifted into a zone-like state at 8:40 or so. I had a sense something was terribly wrong. I woke again at 10:00. Switched on my laptop and connected to the Web. Saw the image of the Twin Towers enveloped in flames. For a second, I thought it was some kind of sick joke.

Dazed, I stumbled down the stairs and turned on the TV. Peter Jennings, whose voice is always a smooth stone, sounded scared. "Oh God," I said out loud, "this is no joke." I picked up the phone, called Pennie, as the second Tower tumbled to the ground. The acid in my stomach rose like the cloud of debris I saw on TV.

We babbled a few minutes. Found solace in the rambling. As I hung up the phone, I quickly dialed Maggie's school. I needed to know she was okay. A knee jerk response to a crisis like this. Annoyance pervaded the secretary's voice. She obviously didn't feel the same. How many calls had she gotten like mine? "They're watching it on TV," she said. "They won't be let out early," she said. "Don't know if they'll have drama practice," she said. My stomach lurched, along with the acids. What will I do 'til she gets home?

I glued myself to the TV. Then bolted to the kitchen to escape. I tried some melon. Hoped my favorite fruit would calm me down. Couldn't taste a thing, with planes exploding and people jumping, blazing across the screen. Never occurred to me to turn it off. Shit. Those damn images imprinted on my brain.

I called Pennie again. She invited me over. I shook my head no. It was hard to be alone. But I knew I couldn't leave the house. Had to be here for Maggie.

Phil called. From Montana. He planned to come home tomorrow, but planes are grounded. He tried reaching Ma in NJ. But phone lines to the New York area are tied in knots. We don't talk much, this brother and I. He feels like a lifeline. "So, when you comin' home?" I said. No idea.

By the time I spoke with Len, the day was sinking in. The sound of his voice softened my heart. For the first time, I surrendered to tears.

When Maggie got home, we hugged tightly. I studied her face. This event would change her forever. Rob her of her innocence, more than any man ever could. I wanted to see if that had happened. She only needed to say a few words and I knew it had. She seemed wired, but held together, as she is most of the time.

We watched the news far too long. Ordered out for pizza like a video was being viewed. At times during the day, I was certain that's what I was watching. One of those movies I never go to see. By now, it had sunken in. Tears spilled from my eyes. The dissolving buildings brought back the dissolved marriage. How I longed for Len's arms to ease this horrific pain.

Instead, I went for the pizza. Drove through town to Paisano's. I examined the faces of the people there. Everyone looked so different. Had they really changed or was it me?

Riding back home, I noticed the flags. They hung from telephone poles along the way. Put up for Old Home's Day, an annual August event celebrated in our town. Just a week ago, I felt irked by their continued presence. Tonight, I saw them in a new way. A source of comfort on the lonely ride home.

At 10:00, I ran a hot bath for Mag. Thought she could use it. She cried for an hour when she got out. I dragged a mattress into my bedroom for her. Gathered up all her favorite stuffed animals. She and those animals slept on the floor next to me. I'm afraid her fear may not go away for a long time.

Late: I woke in the middle of the night, feeling the old terror I felt as a child, when A-bombs were being tested in Utah. Visions of air-raid drills—of us kids at St. Joseph's grade school crouching under desks or in the halls—goose stepped inside my head. My heart is cracked open by this event. Grief spills like an open hydrant. When will it end?

MAGGIE September 12, 2001

Fourth period was just starting, when my principal, Mr. O, came on the loud speaker and announced that terrorists had just flown two planes into the World Trade Center. Everyone was crowded around the speaker, silent and shaking. Miss Filler turned on the TV in time for us to see the towers collapse. I went numb. Then I felt sick. I was torn between crying and throwing up. Instead, I just sat and watched the planes crash into balls of fire, over and over again. We actually tried to make a couple of jokes—what about, I can't remember now.

For the rest of the day, the TVs were on constantly, even during lunch. By the time sixth period rolled around, we were discussing the politics of it all. The whole situation felt so out of place, but it distracted me from the TV for a while. And that image. Those two beautiful buildings, collapsing in on themselves.

Mom cried a lot. I couldn't at first. But it hurt to breathe. I felt sick as I climbed in bed. Mom gave me a back-rub. That's when it started. First a few tears, then some more, then some more. I screamed and sobbed. I couldn't stop. So many thoughts came out of my mouth. Was I going to die? Were any people still alive in the wreckage? How could people hate us so much? Why do I deserve to live? I spent the night in Mom's room. On a mattress on the floor. Surrounded by stuffed animals I hadn't touched in years.

I didn't go to school today. Instead, stayed home and watched the news.

Down they go. The world will never be the same. The US has been attacked and we are no longer safe. I have had one of those times when the 'immortal moment' has happened. Like, where were you when Kennedy was shot or when Princess Diana died? I will always remember I was in calculus class when the Twin Towers fell in on themselves and thousands of people died.

CAROL Wednesday, September 12

I finally got through to Ma. Her voice calmed me down. Sui and Phil are in North Carolina. Too far away. We talked awhile. I need them to get home. Soon!

MAGGIE September 13

Back in school today. Everything's normal. People were joking, worrying about homework, and sleeping through class. It felt so wrong. Shouldn't people be mourning, raging or something? Everyone's so detached. I don't even know if any of my friends cried. And I couldn't bring myself to talk about it. As if there was this understood rule that it shouldn't be mentioned. And I wasn't going to be the one to break it.

CAROL Saturday, September 15

I was appalled when the patrolman pulled me over. "Do you know why I stopped you?" he said. I gave him a dirty look. Why aren't you hunting down terrorists, I wanted to say. Instead, I gave him my license. As I rifled through my purse, searching for my registration, he tapped his foot on the pavement. I cried as I handed him the document. That's when it hit me. This was the same cop who stopped me last spring. Caught me rolling through a stop sign after my carport collapsed. He actually had my new car towed after discovering my registration had expired. Bastard.

"Do you remember me?" I made the mistake of asking.

"Yeah," he said. "You're the one who tried to manipulate me with tears a few months ago." A fury rose in my throat.

"Do you recall what happened this week," I cried out.

"We all feel bad," he said.

"I've been a single mom for 12 years and doing this alone right now is just too much," I blubbered.

"I'm a single dad," he said. I hardly heard him. The tears had managed to wend their way into my ears. I looked him square in the eyes.

"Do you think you can give me a hug?" I said.

"Listen, I'm not gonna give you a ticket," he said. "I just want you to be safe." I was still crying like a fool.

He fumbled with his pen. Shoved it into his shirt pocket. Gave me back my license and registration. "Did you hear me?" he said. He sounded mad. "I'm not going to give you a ticket!" A huge exclamation point sat at the end of that statement. THIS time, he meant to add. Maggie would have said he sounded mean. I tried one more time.

"Do you think you can give me a hug?" He glanced at me, eyes shifting from left to right, then back again. They finally settled on my face.

"I guess I could do that," he said. I told him I would open the door and get out of the car.

Which I did with great caution. And then, this same officer, who had up-ended me a few months before, wrapped his arms around me and gave me the hug I needed.

MAGGIE September 17

Smoke is still hanging over Manhattan. It's like a cloud, suffocating everyone underneath. One more reminder...

CAROL September ~something

Shit. Just being alive scares me.

MAGGIE September 18

I don't want to turn my light off. Is this what life's going to be like now? Being afraid of the dark? If it is, then they really did win.

CAROL Thursday, September 20

I've been talking to Ma every night. We've never done this before. We are connected by fear and pain. The bond we have is fierce. I want to put it in a safe place and save it forever.

chapter eight

Life As We Know It ... The End

CAROL Monday, September 24

We're going to the wedding. Made reservations with Orbitz. Flying into Baltimore on US Airways, then renting a car from there. I told Maggie we can't let the terrorists win. We have to live our lives. Am I nuts for flying now? Sure feels like it. I called Kathy and Jimmy, who live outside of DC, and we'll stay with them our first night.

We also went to Sears, to get Maggie's senior pictures taken. A good break from the insanity. She looked so beautiful. This woman-child of mine. Of course, I cried. What an embarrassment I am!

CAROL Wednesday, September 26

Maggie got her braces put on. I sat next to her for two hours while they glued the damn things to her teeth. She looks like a kid again. They gave her a T-shirt. A frog wearing braces grins on the back. She still needs to get four teeth pulled. We get to go back to that cute oral surgeon.

MAGGIE September 26

Braces suck.

MAGGIE September 28

Woot! I just got my first paper back from Mercus! "A," baby! I love *The Age of Innocence*. It was such a heartbreaking novel. I've always been drawn to books with unhappy endings. *Age of Innocence, Wurthering Heights, Ethan Frome*—all about a love that can never be. I'm not sure why I'm drawn to these stories. Maybe a hope that by reading them I'll be prepared for any pain that comes in my life. I don't know.

But at least it wasn't a heartbreaking grade. What an awesome way to start the school year. Another reason I love Mercus' class: I've always done well in it. Too bad the rest of the world is so totally messed up.

CAROL Friday, October 5

I went to Fleet Bank. To apply for a home equity line of credit. I'm sinking deeper and deeper into debt. I'll need to get millions for the house when I sell it.

That newspaper guy in Florida died from Anthrax. Now we have to worry about being poisoned. Shit. Will it never end?!!

MAGGIE October 5

I don't know what everyone was thinking. Who the hell would put anthrax in an 800 student high school in the middle of Western Mass? It turned out the anthrax was powder from a doughnut, but Mrs. Irving didn't know that. She freaked out. The whole school was evacuated. HazMat was called in. The whole deal. It took over an hour before we could go back inside. Everyone was on the field surrounding a cop car that was summoned.

MAGGIE October 6

I've been noticing something recently, and I really hate it. Having lived so close to an air force base has made me used to jets flying overhead. But ever since Sept. 11, I flinch whenever they fly over the house. I'm not sure if it's because of what they represent, or a fear they're not our planes. Maybe a little of both.

I hate that something I never used to think about has become paramount now. I hate how this paranoia has become innate. I hate that I view everything and everyone so differently. I hate that I hate.

CAROL Sunday, October 7

As missiles attacked Afghan targets, Maggie and I went to see *A Chorus Line* at City Stage. It didn't seem right, but we already had tickets. I felt so confused. We fought on the way to the theater. We sang on the way home. I feel sick to my stomach.

MAGGIE October 7

"Kiss today goodbye, the sweetness and the sorrow...." I love that song. We sang it last year in chorus. Mom and I sang it on the way home. Mom cried.
  "War. What is it good for? Absolutely nothin'...."

CAROL Friday, October 12

Now they think another newspaper guy in Florida has been exposed to anthrax. If we don't go down in the plane, I fear we'll die from that stupid powder. I think I'll start wearing my yellow rubber gloves when I fetch the mail.

MAGGIE October 14

I've never been to Washington. I'm so excited. Of course, it would be better to go when there's a Democrat in the White House, but still....
  We just spent the last half hour circling all the sites we want to see on the map. The Lincoln Memorial, the Washington Memorial, the Vietnam Wall, the Jefferson Memorial, the Capitol Building, the White House, Arlington National Cemetery ... This is going to be great.

CAROL Monday, October 15

Some of that anthrax got mailed to Tom Brokaw. Tom Daschle's office too. I hate this! Seeing those guys in the white suits on the news freaks me out. Nobody's safe. I think I'll wear my rubber gloves to bed. Shit. I better stop watching the news.

Thank goodness Nancy got me into this transformational breathing. I'm freaking out about the craziness out there. Not to mention this trip on Thursday. I must be out of my mind. If I weren't doing this breathing every day, god knows how I'd be. Maggie would surely want to strangle me.

MAGGIE October 16

God, I hope the plane doesn't crash.

CAROL Thursday, October 18

Thank God for Sominex. I actually slept a few hours. Pennie drove us to Bradley. She deserves a medal. I was a basket case. Pennie cracked jokes to fend off my fear. By the time we got to the security check, my knees were ready to buckle.

The flight to Baltimore was fine. No box cutters. No explosions. Not even any turbulence. Except for the stuff inside me. I was never so glad to be on the ground. I wanted to kiss it like the Pope does. Maggie would have landed on death row for killing me, so I resisted the urge.

MAGGIE October 17

Despite the fact that I knew there would be heightened security when we landed in Baltimore, I was still shocked to see armed military guards patrolling the airport. With automatic weapons. I've never seen a real gun before.

Mom and I hung out waiting for Len's flight. We sat there about twenty minutes before we found out, Joe [Len's brother], was sitting right behind us. Also waiting for Len. He'd just gotten in from California. Len, Anna, and Luke were so surprised to see their welcoming committee. They didn't know Mom and I would be there. A mini family reunion at the airport. Cool.

CAROL Friday, October 19

Staying with Kathy and Jimmy was like being home. It was so good to see them. Reminded me of high school. They're like family, such great old friends of Sui's and mine. They provided us a safe haven for this trek we're taking in this war-torn time. Shoot, I must be out of my mind.

The capital was eerie. Monuments were closed—streets blocked off with concrete barriers. Mag and I stopped at Arlington National Cemetery, and the grief I felt from seeing all those head stones—row upon row of dead soldiers—overwhelmed me. I'm an open wound these days. The pain of war stands saluting on my chest.

Maggie lost it with me. "Mom, do you have to do that here?" She wasn't kidding.

"What could be a more appropriate place," I barked.

"I'm just tired of seeing you cry." I did it so much when she was young.

We walked up to Kennedy's grave, separately. I couldn't stop the tears. I sat by his eternal light and sobbed. For all the years I held it back. Like Maggie does now that she's a teen.

We met Len, Anna, Luke and Joe at the Vietnam Veterans Memorial. Joe was in a rage. He's still mad at the war. I needed to get away from him. My eyes were blurry and I stumbled on the cobblestone path, staring at the glossy black granite, mired in all the names, relishing the fact this powerful memorial was designed by a woman.

I looked for Tommy Meade's name. A friend from high school, killed when he was 19. There he was, standing guard, on line 62, panel 37 E. I made a rubbing to take home.

The kids wanted to see the Washington Monument. Joe agreed to take them up. To give Len and I some time. I sensed Len needed to be alone, but stayed with him anyway. I needed his company.

Turned out, the monument was closed. We also found out they'd be towing cars soon. Uncertain if our parking spots were included in this round-up, we ran the distance back to our cars. Sept. 11 is still palpable in this city. I wanted to go home. But we're here for the haul.

We got lost leaving DC. The chaos of rush hour made things worse. The day was still young, unfolding in ways that made me cringe.

We checked into our hotel at St. Mary's City, planning to meet at 7:00. For a big family get-together at Benihana. Sounded like fun. Len thought he should take his kids to Wendy's. I talked him out of it. I wanted him to eat with us. What a mistake!

The wait at the restaurant was long. It was late. His kids were cranky. We all were. Len yelled at the hostess. He was freaking out from today. I learned later that memories from Vietnam overwhelmed him. I'd never seen him like this. He stepped outside. I reassured the kids.

We crowded around a table. Drinks were flowing. Len sat next to me and ordered a carafe of Sake. He never drinks in front of me. An agreement we have. I didn't do well. My turn to freak out. I ran to the bathroom. To catch my breath. Alcohol…

I went back to the table. Tried to be cool. No fucking way that was gonna happen. I was trapped in a sea of drunken relatives. I wanted to go home. Instead, I fought with Len.

CAROL Saturday, October 20

This was such a mistake. This morning I told Len I couldn't keep seeing him if he won't stick to his agreements. This one's really important to me. I won't be with him when he drinks. I am crazy mad. Mad at him for being a jerk, mad at my parents for being alcoholics, mad at everyone who's drinking, mad about Vietnam, mad at Rickey for leaving us, mad about the world we live in. I blubbered once again.

MAGGIE October 20

The wedding was so beautiful. It was in a field by a lake. The sun was shining and everyone was happy. Aidan and Diadra got married in bare feet.

CAROL Sunday, October 21

This was a bad idea. What ever made me think I could do this? Getting our families together at a time like this? I couldn't enjoy the wedding. Len ignored me most of the day. I left Maryland without saying good-bye.

MAGGIE October 22

Back to school and the real world. And let's face it, the real world really bites.

CAROL Wednesday, October 24

The Postmaster General announced "there is no guarantee that the mail is safe." What's with this guy? Geez! Let's get the masses *really* scared. Tell them we can't guarantee you won't find that nasty little powder in your mailbox! Get bent, will you!

CAROL Thursday, October 25

The Airborne Express guy stopped by with my contract. For my book. Oh my god. I have no idea what this means. It's ten pages long.

AGREEMENT, entered into as of October 11, 2001 between **SIMON & SCHUSTER, INC.** ("Publisher"), 1230 Avenue of the Americas, New York, New York 10020, **CAROL WEIS,** ("Author") …

Author. That's me. Look Ma, they called me author!

MAGGIE October 25

Shut the damn news off. I'm sick of this shit.

CAROL Friday, October 26

I called Stephan and asked if he'd look over the contract. I've combed through it a few times, but it reads like Russian to me. I made copies and wrote some questions for him. "Is 5% what I'll receive on retail only? Who has control here? Do I not have any say in who gets my work?" I love the part about theme park rights. Let's see, what will we call it? Ida Mae's A-moos-ments?! I am starring in my own dream.

CAROL Saturday, October 27

Trina and I went to Green Street Cafe. We go all out for our birthdays. To-night, we started off with a mix of delicate greens with warm chevre and wal-nuts, followed by tenderloin of beef drenched in gorgonzola butter for Trina, while I treated myself to loin lamb chops, with a mustard beurre blanc. Trina couldn't resist the Crème Brûlée, and I endured a rich chocolate torte with raspberry sauce scribbled across the plate. Afterwards, we waddled to our cars and hugged good-bye. We're happy our birthdays fall so close to each other. And happy to take a break from reality.

CAROL Thursday, November 1

I can't write. Except for this journal. After what's happened, nothing else seems important enough to put down on paper. I want to work on my novel. It feels disrespectful to even think about it. Besides, there's nothing that wants to be written. No room for any story but that one September day.

MAGGIE November 1

Halloween sucked this year. Especially since the last few years have been so much fun. How could staying home, handing out candy, possibly compete with blowing up a pumpkin? That year was my introduction to the pyromaniac side of my guy friends. In their infinite wisdom, Chris, Jack, Mel and Joe decided it'd be cool to light a pumpkin on fire. So they hollowed it out, filled it w/lighter fluid, and threw a match on it.

Only problem was, they put too much fluid in it, so it spilled all over the place. It left a trail going up to Nat's wooden deck. So the pumpkin exploded and went flying into the woods. And the flames started to follow the trail back to the house. We all freaked out. And rather than getting some water to put it out, Jack tried to smother it by using his stocking feet. Yeah, that wasn't one of his brighter moments. They finally got the fire out, by slapping the flames w/ a snow shovel. My boys are so smart. And how sad is it that I miss almost burning the house down!!

MAGGIE November 4

I came across a copy of W.H. Auden's "Funeral Blues" today and wept. I was so embarrassed, even though no one saw me. Now that I think about it, I cried when it was read in *Four Weddings and a Funeral* too, so it wasn't that odd. It's a beautiful poem. One of my favorites. I'd love to have it read at my funeral. Can you really request something like that? It would have to be someone who was as moved as I am and wanted to read it. It can't be my idea, can it? I wonder how many times it's been read in the last two months. Maybe I don't like it so much, after all...

CAROL Monday, November 5

Len called. The sound of his voice makes me livid. The sound of his voice makes me melt. I have not forgiven him. It's the alcohol. I hate this. I really wish I could drink. A scotch would be good. I always hated scotch. What a lie. I would drink anything put in front of me.

MAGGIE November 5

Saw Mr. Garth today. He's such a dork. He reminded me of the deadlines for my college applications. Like I don't know. Vassar and BU—Jan. 1; BC—Jan 3; Skidmore, Mt. Holyoke and UMass—Jan 15. I really don't want to go to UMass!

CAROL Tuesday, November 6

This anger towards Len is full of past betrayals with him *and* other men. A trunk-load of broken agreements. I wanted to slam the phone in his ear. I told him I'm not ready to forgive him. I'm not ready to forgive myself for putting up with all the betrayals for all those years. Len's is only one. The affair Rickey had is also in the mix of fury I feel. Maybe I should break this off for good.

Men suck. I hate them all. I hate myself even more. I'd really like a drink.

MAGGIE November 7

Boys suck. They are horrible, manipulative creatures who should be shot. 'Cause a boy hurt my friend. Evil boy. Stay away from Jeanne. Poor Jeanne. This guy from her water-skiing team she's had a crush on forever. Since way before she and Jack got together. And he's been the first one to show interest in her since she and Jack broke up.

But the other day, I got this mammoth email from her, all about this guy.

This boy, who is pressuring her to sleep w/him—god, all they've done is flirt w/each other—and now he wants sex. And Jeanne was actually thinking of doing it. It's so unfair. I've been hearing for years about this guy. And it's because of that, she's considering it.

So of course, I wrote back to her, screaming, (as much as you can in an email), "don't do it. This asshole should not be the first person you sleep with. I know you'll regret it. I don't want you to become one of those clichéd stories about girls who give it up and wish they didn't."

Not Jeanne, who I've known since kindergarten. Thankfully, I think she'll listen to me. I'm still waiting to hear back from her. It's the first time she'll have seen him since she wrote to me. Good luck, sweetie.

MAGGIE November 8

Living life in peace
—John Lennon

I see the end of the world,
I can see how this will end.
The power that corrupts binds us.
But even the strongest chain can be broken.
Melted away, into a ring, that joins us.
One moment, when all that remains is joy.
And then, the end.
The greatest irony of them all.
Peace shall come,
But it will be too late.
And the tears shall wash away the sins of the past
In a river that sweeps the Earth.

CAROL Friday, November 9

How will I ever get through this college application thing with Maggie? I want to control every step of the way. She wants to kill me each time I open my mouth. How will I ever get through this college application thing alive?

MAGGIE November 9

I've gotta work on my college essay. Except I have absolutely no idea what to write. I'm coming up completely blank. What the hell am I gonna write about?

CAROL Saturday, November 10

I sign on   after seeing a
flic with my daughter   and
hear the customary chorus
'you've got mail' ring 'round
the room and there ~~you~~ standing
watch   over my mailbox is
JerseyMarine19   and I wonder

if Karma   for pushing pacifism
during this terrorist war   is
catching up with me.
Discovering it's my high
school heartthrob   my pulse
soars to adolescent heights
and I hear ~~the~~ a girl group croon
'Baby Love'   as we whirl around
the glossy surface of ~~a~~ hardwood
gymnasium floor   glistening eyes
taking in the promise   of things
we couldn't give   and when
he pulls me close   his ~~warm~~
breath   on my neck
is enough.

Why, Frank Lieb. You ol' cutie. Boy, was I sweet on you in high school. So you found me on Classmates.com. What a nice surprise. After all these years. Perfect timing, Frank!

MAGGIE   November 12

Oh, thank God Jeanne listened to me. And told the bastard off. And as if braces weren't enough, now I have to get four teeth pulled. Which means two days off from school.

MAGGIE   November 15

Dr. Cappetta woke me up from surgery singing, *"Wake up, Maggie, I think I've got something to say to you..."* He's so sweet.

Ice packs are my friends. I have them on both sides of my face. I'm eating baby food again. Four of those babies came out today.

CAROL   Monday, November 19

I heard from Frank again. He told me he's sober too. For twenty years now. Was he sent to cheer me up? As the days grow darker, so do I. Remember deary, he's married.

MAGGIE November 20

Got my SAT scores. 640/verbal, 610/math, 700 on my writing sample. Yay!

MAGGIE November 25

Mom and I celebrated turkey day with Lauren and Joe. Aunt Susie and Uncle Phil went to New Jersey to see Ma. We wanted to stay in Mass. The best part was seeing *Harry Potter and the Sorcerer's Stone* with Lauren. She's a Harry Potter freak like me. The theater was packed. We sat up close. Lauren and I were in our glory. Daniel Radcliffe is so cute. I feel like a pedophile saying that. I just can't wait to see the next one. *The Chamber of Secrets.*

Lauren was the one who got me into Harry Potter. I was determined to avoid the books, but the last time we visited them in Boston, she convinced me to start reading HP. Said I had to read at least three chapters. I did, then couldn't stop. I read the last one in a night. Couldn't put it down. They're written for children, but they don't read like they are. J.K. Rowling has created a whole new world, the same way J.R.R. Tolkien did fifty years ago. And who wouldn't want to play quidditch?

CAROL Wednesday, November 28

My first advance check came from Simon & Schuster. $1,250. I went to the bank to deposit it. I should have been ecstatic. My first big check as a writer. Instead, I cried.

MAGGIE November 30

If Mom doesn't leave me alone about the damn applications and essay, I'm going to shoot her. *"Bang bang, I shot her down, bang bang, she hit the ground..."*

CAROL Friday, Nov 30

Yesterday   George Harrison died
they played Beatles A to Z for
12 hours on rock 102 and as
each love song   squirmed its
way   through the speaker   a ~~nother~~
nother cookie crammed itself
into my mouth.   I'm running
an experiment   want to see
how much junk food it takes
to fill the ~~canyon~~ gorge that's been
gouged in the cellar of my
stomach.   So far   no hostess
twinkie   no hot fudge sundae
no chili dog   no fist sized chunk
of fucking chocolate is big enough
to fill the gaping hole the conflict
of loving you creates.   May a gob
of freshly chewed bubblegum
stick to the bottom   of your
favorite shoe   as you enter
the home of your most
treasured client.

I can't let go of this thing with Len. Anger or love. It's so freaking annoying. *Something in the way he moves, attracts me like no other lover…* I'd really like a drink.

Better get to a meeting.

MAGGIE December 1

Mom and I cut down the Christmas tree. And hauled it home. I think I'm getting tired of this tradition. Too much work. Why can't she just buy one like Dad does?

CAROL Monday, December 3

He's gone The quiet one. Dead at 58. The mystical force behind the band that rocked my youth. A piece of me goes with him. Along with millions of others my age. And now my heart gently weeps.

I was a ~~mere~~ sophomore in high school when The Beatles first came to America. We were in the ~~middle~~ throws of our annual fund raising extravaganza that brought in thousands of dollars for our private parochial school. That year it was Fiorello – a musical based on the life of another popular New York City mayor. The tenth grade chorus was singing "I Love a Cop." As ~~it~~ was the case each year, we were stashed in a classroom the entire night until it was our turn to appear onstage.

Sister Juanita Maria had the ~~good fortune~~ misfortune of being in charge of us that fateful Sunday night. It was about 7:53pm when Sister ~~Juanita~~ made the mistake of stepping out of the classroom. Exactly what my friends and I had prayed for. We'd been planning our escape all week. As soon as our classroom monitor disappeared, we would too. Beth Dougherty's TV room was our destination. She lived about a mile from school. We might not make it in time for Ed's ceremonious opening "Ladies and gentlemen. Tonight we have for you a really, really big shew," but as long as we ~~laid eyes on~~ saw those darling mop-heads, we didn't care.

After sneaking down the hall and out the rear entrance of the yellow brick building, we raced coatless down Valley Road to Beth's house. ~~Breathless~~ Gasping upon arrival, we settled onto the carpet just in time to hear the Fab Four sing their opening tunes. "All My Loving", "Till There was You", and "She Loves You" had us screaming far louder than Beth's parents could stand. With each shake of their heads, we screamed even louder. By the time Ed called them back for their finishing numbers of "I Saw Her Standing There" and "I Want to Hold Your Hand," Beth's parents were nowhere to be found.

We took our time getting back to school—all of us talking at the same time. Giggling with a profusion of passion and joy only adolescents ~~can~~ get to share. We knew we'd be in trouble, but we didn't care. We had just captured a moment in time that even then we knew would become a legend.

When it was our time to go on stage that night, even though the words "I love a cop, I love a cop" seeped through my lips, I wasn't thinking about any officer of the law at that time. I was gaga over George, the quiet one, whose guitar ~~today~~ on this day gently weeps.

I wrote this in my journal, but it ended up on NPR.

CAROL Sunday, December 9

I am sinking into a hole. This bottomless well. The tar pit of depression. I've started to go back to bed after Maggie goes to school. Oh god. This is scary. But it feels so good.

I hate the lack of light this time of year. As Sarah sings, "And oh, darkness, I feel like letting go…" Thoughts of suicide teeter on the ridgepole of my brain. It feels like slow quick sand. It's way too familiar. That's what scares me. Like I felt when Rickey left. But not. It's different, but the same. It terrifies me. Cripes, the friggin' *Pause*. And Len.

CAROL Monday, December 10

Kristi Ceccarossi from the *Gazette* came to interview me about my children's book with Simon & Schuster. She was young and vivacious. Her enthusiasm was contagious, so the interview went well. Hot stuff!

MAGGIE December 10

We're seniors. And we're going out with a bang. Starting with "Deck the Halls." We are so going to win the hall design contest. Our hallway looks incredible. Today a bunch of us stayed late and covered each locker with wrapping paper, a bow and name tag. We have a hundred lockers that look just like Christmas presents. And we made a giant Christmas Tree and Menorah to hang on the wall. All that's left is to hang the lights. 2002 kicks ass!

CAROL Tuesday, December 11

Maggie had her winter concert tonight. They sang one of my favorite hymns (my favorite version on the next page). I used to sing it to Maggie when I tucked her in at night. Sui and Phil came down. Rickey was there. They chatted with him at intermission, while I stood by and seethed. I don't want to share them right now. Plus, I'm mad at him. Mag still eats alone when she goes to his house. After all I've said to him. And he gives me such a hard time about the cost of schools she's applying to. Like it's my fault. Shit. He hasn't taken her to see one friggin' college!

Let there be peace on earth
and let it begin with me,
Let there be peace on earth
the peace that was meant to be,
With Earth as our Mother,
we are Family,
Let us walk with each other
in perfect harmony.
Let peace begin with me,
let this be the moment now,
With every step I take,
let this be my solemn vow,
To take each moment,
and live each moment in peace eternally,
Let there be peace on earth,
and let it begin with me.

MAGGIE December 12

Vassar wants a writing sample. An analytical essay from 11th or 12th grade. What should I send? Oh god. They also want me to write 3 paragraphs about the co-curricular and work experiences that has had the most impact on me. My mind's a blank. What the hell should I write?!

Won't someone just hit me on the head and put me out of my misery? These applications are consuming my life! Can't I have just five minutes to enjoy my last year of high school? Is that really too much to ask?

CAROL Thursday, December 13

Maggie's not gonna have those freakin' applications done on time. I've been down to her room at least a hundred times tonight. I want to pull out her eye lashes. Bend her fingers back to her wrists. I want to scream in her bloody ears. I just want her to get the damn things done. Grrr. I think it gives her great pleasure to see me like this.

MAGGIE   December 13

Go *a-way*, Mom!

CAROL   Friday, December 14

Kevin Gutting was here to take my photo for the article about "The Day the Cows Got Loose." I think he took some good shots. I hope he did. This is so weird. Pinch me. I must be dreaming.

MAGGIE   December 16

College essay. Mr. Mercus says personal is good. O.K.

   I was three years old when I developed my biggest fear. It wasn't from a movie or a television show. Just a brief sentence uttered by my babysitter; "If you get out of bed one more time, your room will catch on fire." I know she didn't ~~mean or~~ intend for me to take it literally. She used the threat to make me stay in bed. But the harsh tone of her voice, combined with the blazing red of my carpet, the fear permeated my being. That night, and for many thereafter, I dreamed about dying in a fire. One of the most vivid I ~~can~~ remember was in second grade. The school caught on fire, and everyone escaped but me. They climbed out the windows while I was frozen in place, my feet were glued to the floor. The flames crept closer and closer, and I couldn't move.
   For years this fear plagued me. It increased tenfold with my parent's divorce. After my father left, my mother and I lived alone in our large, wooden, far-too-combustible house. I lost the sense of stability and safety I felt when my dad lived with us. For months, I spent nights ~~sleeping~~ huddled in my mom's bed, desperately seeking the safe haven my room wouldn't provide.
   Not only did this fear affect my sleeping patterns, it influenced how and where we lived. When my parents split up, my father made sure to rent an apartment that had a bedroom with a fire escape. Of course, that room was mine.
   I also became obsessed about appliances. I asked my mother every night if she turned off the oven or unplugged the toaster. Although my mother rarely ironed clothes, I found myself worrying about the iron. I had stomachaches for years. My life seemed ruled by a debilitating sense of dread.
   My fear began to dissipate when I finally told my mother what happened

when I was three. She cried and stomped around the house for days. She wanted to call the girl who threatened me, but I wouldn't let her. Telling ~~the story~~ my mom was sufficient. Once I got old enough to take care of myself, and wasn't forced to rely on my parents for my safety ~~anymore~~, I felt more secure. Even now, years later, the sound of a siren from a distant fire truck sends chills down my spine.

What will they think of me if I send this in? Do I sound too immature? Ack! I have no idea what's appropriate for a college essay.

CAROL Tuesday, December 18

The article about my children's book is in today's *Gazette*. I went to Extra-Mart and bought 10 copies. The photo is good. And she turned our interview into a decent piece of writing.

"Revisiting my experiences is the best part. You get to manipulate memories, so they turn out the way you want."

It's so bizarre. Having my words quoted in a newspaper. Getting positive attention. If only Sister Juanita could see me now! I worked so hard at getting her to notice me. It's all I knew how to do. Be a pest so she'd get angry. This is so foreign to me.

MAGGIE December 19

I am *so* freaking out about these applications. Can't think of anything else towrite. I guess I'll send *The Age of Innocence* paper to Vassar. I've got to have BU, BC and Vassar's into Mr. Garth tomorrow. I have a headache and I want to puke. And if Mom doesn't leave me alone, someone may get murdered tonight. ACK!!

CAROL Wednesday, December 19

I wonder if someone can get arrested for sticking uncooked spaghetti in someone's ears while they're sleeping. Or gluing their eyelids shut, or pulling their toenails off. I'm thinking about doing this to Maggie. I don't actually want to kill her, just want to maim her. This college application thing has pushed me over the edge. How is that possible? I'm already there. I think I'm losing my mind. And don't know if I'll find it again. *AAAAAAAA!!*

chapter nine

Sparknotes, Ack!

MAGGIE December 24

Mom and I cooked tonight. Mom reminded me that this is my last Christmas home. I mean living here full time. She's like all, "but this is our last" whatever we do now. She's trying to make me sad like her. No way I'm going there. The soufflé actually came out well. Yay me. I made a soufflé.

CAROL Monday, December 24

Maggie and I made our cheese soufflé. Our Christmas Eve tradition.

CAROL Wednesday, December 26

We spent Christmas at Sui's and Phil's. Ma was there. She's starting to give things away. Gave me her string of pearls, the ones I loved as a child, and the antique portrait of the bare-breasted maiden. Plus the small ones of her younger sister's. The ones that sat on our coffee table for years. I'm scared. I can't think of Ma dying yet. I've just gotten her back in my life.

MAGGIE December 26

Mom ruined Christmas. She told everyone to give me money, so while Aunt Susie handed out all the presents, I sat there with my little money envelopes.

It really sucked.

CAROL Tuesday, January 1, 2002

I hung our new calendar in the kitchen. One with quotes by Thich Nh t Hanh. The Vietnamese Buddhist monk and peace activist. I thought it might help us through this year. We'll need it. Plus, today I'm 12-years sober! Wow!

MAGGIE January 2

Braces suck big time. Forget about ever having sex for the next three years. This is all Mom's fault. I'm stuck with being a fucking virgin.

CAROL Thursday, January 3

I brush against you   ~~through~~
out the day   stumbling over
snippets of time we've spent
alleviating ~~our~~ appetites
on weekend trysts.   Just
yesterday   while shifting
piles of paper   from room to
room   a business card surfaced
corners curled from careless
neglect   our nibbles in ~~new~~
new london   a remote
repast.   That night   sitting
across from you   a booth   in a
barren chinese cafe   ~~my~~ eyes linked
whispering of prior affections
the taste of your fervor   loitering
on my lustrous lips   eager for much
more   than the fortune cookie's
tantalizing   asian cuisine.

I miss Len. I must be forgiving him. I want to be in his arms.

MAGGIE January 3

If Mom knocks on my door one more time tonight, she's a dead woman. Leave me alone. I will get the applications done. In my time, not yours. Bug off, will you!!

CAROL Friday, January 4

I had a long conversation with Kevin. We talked about possible illustrators. He's thinking about Kathryn Brown or Matt Faulkner. Kathryn has worked with Jane Yolen and Cynthia Rylant. I swoon at the notion. He asked me to check out their work.

   He also wants me to change a few things in the manuscript. Not much. He's funny and gentle, and respectful of my writing. He thinks we should change the title. I resist the idea. He tells me about a book called *The Day the Goose Got Loose*. It's ten years old, but may still be remembered. Written by Reeve Lindbergh. How can I compete with her? He mentions "When the Cows Got Loose" for ours. Says it fits the action of the story better. I still resist. But find our conversation fascinating. I'm in a whole new world.

MAGGIE January 7

Today was the first meeting about the trip to Europe this summer. Mrs. Hart said we will definitely visit Paris and Madrid. Other than that, we're not sure where else. I just want to go to Paris. Climb the Eiffel Tower. Tour the Louvre. See Notre Dame. Walk through the Hall of Mirrors at Versailles.

CAROL Wednesday, January 9

I have an appointment at Woronoco Savings tomorrow. To refinance the house. Gulp.

MAGGIE January 9

God! Can't Mom shut up for one minute about my applications? Tonight she actually kicked my door. What's her problem? Does she really think I would screw myself over by not doing them in time? Hello. I do actually want to go to college.

CAROL Thursday, January 10

They turned me down. My trust is being challenged, and my foot is killing me. I'm being punished. We will not starve. We will get by. As I sink deeper and deeper into debt, it's hard to trust. Repeat after me. I trust the process of life. Everything I need is always provided. I am safe. The universe takes care of me. Say it ten times. Now believe it.

MAGGIE January 10

I gave idiot Garth the applications for Skidmore, Mt. Holyoke, and Dad's favorite, UMass. It's out of my hands now. I just hope I get into one of the schools I applied to. Actually, I don't really give a rat's ass today. I have an English paper due tomorrow. Don't know how I'm gonna pull it off. I get one thing done and there's something else. Is this ever going to end? I may need to resort to SparkNotes.com.

MAGGIE January 11

I don't know what the hell Natasha is thinking. Is she trying to destroy any chance of success in the future? She needs to finish her applications. Actually, she's already too late for one. Bennington's deadline has come and gone. And Hampshire's up in a few days. That leaves UMass.

What's so difficult about filling out a couple of applications? If only Peter was like Mom, she'd do them only to stop the nagging. I guess I'll have to step up the harassing. This will end two ways. Either she gets them done with some helpful encouragement from me or I'll kill her with my whining. Should be fun either way.

MAGGIE January 13

Found a wallpaper for my desktop that has two of my favorite things in the world. Michael Vartan and "Funeral Blues." Together. That just totally made my day.

CAROL Wednesday, January 16

Maggie came home really upset. She went straight to her room without saying boo. She's never done that before. I sensed she needed some time alone, but couldn't help myself. I made my way up the stairs and stood by her door, listening to her cry. I knocked and went in. She spilled the beans. Mr. Mercus accused her of plagiarizing her latest English paper. Along with two other girls. "He's really mad, Mom. And I feel so bad I disappointed him."

I feel so powerless. My heart is breaking for her.

MAGGIE January 17

Mr. Mercus said he's going to withdraw his letters of recommendation from the colleges. Shit. I am *so* screwed. If I don't get into school, Mom and Dad are gonna kill me. This really sucks bad. I mean really bad. And the worst part is, I have no one to blame but myself. And damn SparkNotes.com.

Class is completely unbearable. I can't look Mercus in the eye anymore. And to think he used to be my favorite teacher. And I was one of his favorite students. Not anymore. He hates me. I just want to curl into a ball and cry. And never go to school again.

CAROL Friday, January 18

I called Mr. Mercus today. Wanted to get his side of the story.

"Gary, don't you think you're being a little too harsh?" I told him how stressed she'd been. He wouldn't budge. I lost it and broke into tears, then hung up the phone. Shit.

Fail her, yes. But withdraw your recommendations? And I can't get mad at Maggie after the year we've had. I feel profoundly grateful she hasn't turned to drugs.

At least I think she hasn't turned to drugs. Oh god. What if she has? Snorting coke while I'm sleeping in the next room. Sneaking out the window to meet her 30-year-old drug dealer. Who's also her lover. The one she met online. When she was twelve!

Oh cripes. Give me a break. STOP IT RIGHT NOW!

MAGGIE January 18

I hate Dad. He's as bad as Mr. Mercus. He's actually standing up for him. My own father. He says he'd do the same thing if one of his students did what I did. Does he forget that I'm his daughter? Yeah, I messed up. But does he really have to condemn me for life? I can't take this much longer.

MAGGIE January 20

Still not talking to Dad.

CAROL Monday, January 21

I broke down and called Rickey. At home. In spite of the chance of talking to Teresa. Her hate for me hurtles through the wires of the phone.

I gave him a piece of my mind. Told him he better find some way to support her through this or he may lose her. He said he'd call Mercus. That he would handle it. I think he may have mentioned diplomatically. Some macho thing. So he doesn't think I'm diplomatic? Shit. Not when it comes to our daughter.

MAGGIE January 21

I really screwed up. There's no way to fix this.

CAROL Tuesday, January 22

I had my writer's meeting here tonight. I made copies of Matt Faulkner's and Kathryn Brown's work for Linda, Nancy, and Elaine to see. We scrutinized the art. We think Matt Faulkner would be best. His sense of humor stands out. I will email Kevin about my preference.

I told them about Maggie and Mercus. I also called Marj for advice. She's in college admissions. They all think he's going too far.

MAGGIE January 23

A reporter got kidnapped in Pakistan. Daniel Pearl. From New York.

MAGGIE January 25

Finally talked to Dad. Said he's been leaving messages for Mr. Mercus. That he would talk him out of withdrawing the recommendation letters. I hope he comes through with this. I'm still getting a zero on my paper. I deserve that. But losing his recommendation would kill me. And ruin my chances for college. I know that Mercus wrote the best letter. Well, except for Debbie. But Debbie's wouldn't carry as much weight, since she's not actually my teacher. Oh god. Screwed for life.

CAROL Friday, February 1

I went for my annual breast-smashing today. That machine was undoubtedly invented by a man. I just love how they get your boob pressed flat as a pancake, then ask you to wrap your arm tightly around the friggin' thing and then have the unmitigated gall to run and hide, and say as sweet as maple syrup, "Now relax and breathe." AAAAAAAAAAAAAAAAAA!!

"Okay. All done."

MAGGIE February 2

Today was Ma's birthday and Mom wanted me to sing happy birthday with her on the phone. Like I used to do when I was ten. She just doesn't get that I don't do that stuff anymore.

CAROL Wednesday, February 6

I saw Billy Collins at Smith tonight. My favorite poet for years. Now that he's poet laureate, I have to share him with the entire nation. I'm not sure I like that.

I remember reading his poem "The Best Cigarette," and knew I was in love. How could anyone describe addiction with such panache? Made me want to light up again.

I was disappointed with his reading. Like going out with someone you've had a crush on for years, but you've never heard them speak. You imagine they sound like James Earl Jones. Instead, they sound like Dick Cheney. Fortunately, he read some of my favorite poems.

I gave him one of mine from "DIVORCE PAPERS."

...Stopping at a red light   I succumb
to its advances   and grab ~~the~~ a book from
the Barnes and Noble bag   photos
of Alice Walker and Amy Tan   hug

its contents   as it occupies the passenger
seat   of my car.   I read a poem by Billy
Collins   sucking on the words of his
Osso Bucco   like a calf on a teat   as a

herd of harried drivers   drum fingers
on ~~their~~ steering wheels.   I smile at them
as I bite down on another verb
let its nuances loiter on my tongue

and that's when I notice their fingers
beating out the rhythm of the poem
so I join in   tapping and reading
as the light slinks into green...

Wonder if he's read it?

MAGGIE February 6

No word yet from Dad about my fate. This is *killing* me. I should have just sucked it up and cited SparkNotes. But who ever does that? Would it have *really* made a difference? Hand me the poison now.

CAROL Thursday, February 7

Aunt El and Uncle Chet are both in the hospital. Uncle Chet broke his hip. Aunt El is so nauseous she can't keep any food or water down. They don't know what's wrong with her. Oh God, please let them be okay. And while you're at it, please don't let anything happen to Ma.

CAROL Friday, February 8

I drove Maggie to school today. I fumed the whole way there. I hate that! Having to drive her to school when she misses the bus. You'd think I'd welcome this task with jubilance.

After all, this is her last year at home before going off to college.

I am really fed up with raising this girl alone and want to run through the woods screaming my head off. But it's too damn cold. Grrr!

MAGGIE February 8

Mom went off on one of her woe-is-me-I'm-a-single-parent rants tonight. Like I don't know that she and Dad are divorced. *Hello*. I lived it. I had to deal with her when she was all depressed and messed up.

Like the time she sent me to kindergarten in the morning, instead of the afternoon session. I got to school and I was in the wrong class. I still remember sitting in Mrs. Smith's classroom, with my hood pulled up to hide myself, waiting for Dad, not Mom, to come get me. And when I got home, Mom was lying in bed with all the blinds closed and the lights off, crying. Yeah. Real stable. So she better shut up about having to do everything by herself.

CAROL Monday, February 11

Nancy and I are going to the SCBWI conference in New York. We're staying at The Roosevelt. Peg is driving us down. We are so psyched about this trip. Nancy is helping me with the cost. I feel so supported by my friends right now. I am blessed beyond belief.

CAROL Tuesday, February 12

I got a post card from Billy Collins! "Thanks so much for your poem that has me as a hungry calf. I suppose we all feel like that from time to time."

I'm swooning! You hungry calf, you. No wait! He didn't get it. I'm the hungry calf. Maybe I should call him about this....

MAGGIE February 13

We all knew it was coming, but it was still a shock when Mr. O announced this week that Mrs. Warren had finally succumbed to liver cancer. Even if the way it happened is different, it feels just like Mrs. Chevrette.

Yesterday, we went to her wake in Easthampton. I met her family, who she was always talking about in class. Today was her funeral. Natasha, Jack, Josh and I drove down to West Springfield for her service. The church was filled to the brim. Almost every teacher from Hampshire was there, along w/a bunch of students. The service was beautiful, at least as beautiful as a funeral can be. The quote on the program for the memorial really moved me: "Come to me, all who labor and are heavy laden...and I will give you rest," Matthew 11:28.

After the service, we hung around the church a while. I saw Mr. Mercus talking to some other teachers, but tried to avoid him. I ended up outside, waiting for Jack. All of a sudden, Mr. Mercus came up to me. He told me he decided not to go through on withdrawing his letter of recommendation. In honor of Mrs. Warren. I almost started crying again. I think Mr. Mercus understood, because he left me alone.

CAROL Friday, February 15

I really am starring in a dream. Nancy took a picture of me in front of the Simon & Schuster building. I stared up at the large gold letters above the rotating doors and had to catch my breath. Alyssa is a doll and Kevin is a stitch. We were there for an hour. Sitting in the office of my editor at Simon & Schuster. It will take me years to get over this.

MAGGIE February 16

Okay, it's been a month since I gave the applications to Garth. When am I gonna hear?

CAROL Sunday, February 17

I just got back from New York. This morning, while other attendees learned about promoting their books, I took a subway to Ground Zero. Got off the train at Fulton to a confusion of iron maidens, bolted shut, with no access to the surface.

Finally found my way to the street.

I stood there, in a daze, struck. Stared at the gaping hole where the towers once were. The void was overwhelming. Shaking myself free, I headed towards the river where tickets for the viewing platform were up for grabs. I passed a deli. A construction worker paused to light a cigarette. I turned and asked what it was like, working on the site. He started to ramble. "They told us to leave," he said. "Thought they found a pipe bomb," he said. "The security in this place sucks," he said. "It was okay at the beginning. Now they've gotten too loose. Anyone in a truck can drive through and blow us up." His eyes, reddened from fatigue, shifted back and forth, as he took another drag. Two co-workers emerged from the deli to join him. I asked how many hours a day they put in. "12 to 18," said one. "Seven days a week. " One of them, a gas mask strapped to his head, motioned the others back to work.

MAGGIE February 19

The snow rolls off the roof during the night.
Is it spring yet?

CAROL Wednesday, February 20

I called Sui to tell her about my trip to New York. Len was there with his kids. The nerve! Going to my sister's when I'm still mad at him! Sui asked if I wanted to talk to him. Of course I did. I said, "I guess so." I gushed about my visit to Simon & Schuster. His voice sounded green. I relished the fact. We have reconnected at last.

MAGGIE February 23

Auditions are the *worst things ever.* Especially when the audition is for college, not a play. Why, oh why, do I want to go to BU? At least it's over. And my monologue was from *Midsummer,* so I just used my memories from Cassie's performance for mine.

Besides the audition, we went on a tour of the BU campus. The theater is off-campus, so we took the T to get there. And Amy was on the same train. I haven't seen her since graduation. It was awesome to talk with her. Amy has always been such a laid back and fun person. Who else could have gotten me to dance on a table at the winter cotillion last year? Now that was *big* fun.

The BU theater is haunted. At least that's what they say. But I was definitely getting some weird vibes while we were backstage. It could've been the basic spookiness that exists in every old theater. It's definitely the best venue we've seen for a school so far. Do I really want to major in theater?

MAGGIE February 24

Been thinking about BU. I'm not sure I like the idea of being so isolated in the conservatory there. BC is really the place I'd like to be.

CAROL Monday, February 25

Len called. We bantered back and forth. I asked him what he wants. He fumbled for the words. "Well, I was just thinking that, I don't know, that maybe we could get together sometime." I wanted to shake him. My heart did flips. "Oh, when were you thinking?" I said. He's like a greased pig—really hard to pin down. I kept badgering him for a date. I rubbed off the grease and got him to succumb.

He invited me for next weekend. He's playing the part of Boss in *Of Mice and Men* at Guild Hall in East Hampton. He'd like me to see it. First time he's invited me to Long Island for a weekend since we started seeing each other. I just wonder where this relationship is going!???

MAGGIE February 28

I can think of very few things that are more relaxing than laying back in a dark room while listening to classical music. Add to the fact that the music's live, and you've got it made. It had to be the best period of school. Thank you, Ms. Holt, for not coming to school, so Nat, Jack, Shawn and I could sneak out of chorus and go chill in the auditorium with the lights off. Shawn played "Moonlight Sonata" and "Fur Elise" on the piano. I don't know how he does it. He's a musical genius. I need more days like this one. When will I hear from BC?

CAROL Sunday, March 3

I had a great weekend with Len. Got all decked out for his play. I felt so beautiful when I walked into Guild Hall. I could see it in Len's eyes when he saw me. Was it lust or love?

It was wonderful to see him perform. I could tell he was nervous. 'Cause I was in the audience, of course. We had dinner with Ed and Corrine on Saturday. They went to see Len's play while I stayed home and vegged. While I laid in bed this morning, Len made a fabulous cream cheese and herb omelet. I didn't want to leave. Did I mention the love-making?

Driving away I watch you from
my rearview mirror   as wipers sigh
swishing aside   droplets of rain   that
spill from soggy skies...

MAGGIE March 4

I have this French paper due this week. I so do not want to do it. I love French, the language that is, but I just want to get out of here so badly.

CAROL Wednesday, March 6, 9:30pm

I stumbled out of bed, following a fitful night's sleep, to wake Maggie for school. Like I've done every morning since kindergarten. Bright light tumbled from the crack beneath her door. A sure sign she pulled an all-nighter. Staying up to finish the French paper. How will she ever make it through college? I managed. Suppose she will too.

I opened the door. Lights blared around her room. She was nowhere to be found. I spoke her name. A question mark punctuated it as I turned and headed for the stairs. Maybe she's in the shower. I searched for her. No sign of life anywhere. Did she lose it and suddenly take off? Run through the cornfield naked? Thoughts like this raced through my mind. This year's been tough on her. On all of us, for that matter.

Went back to her room. A blanket from a younger time lay heaped across her bed. I moved in close and proceeded to touch it, stricken with fear. I can see the headlines. "Local teenager dies writing French paper." I'm the one who needs a naked run through the cornfield. I'm afraid the neighbors might shoot me. At the moment, the idea doesn't sound so bad.

I lifted the blanket. Her body, dressed in yesterday's clothes, was curled like a fetus, lying sideways on the bed. I touched her head. My eyes fixed on her breathing. Her shoulder rose and fell like a wave in formation, moving toward the shore. This felt familiar. Like the hours I stood by her crib. Watching to make sure she was still alive. That longing came back. I wanted to hold her hostage. Freeze-frame her. And stare eternally.

MAGGIE March 11

The first time I read this poem, I fell in love w/ it. And had absolutely no idea where it came from. It wasn't until years later that I found out it was by Pablo Neruda. I immediately went out and bought a copy of *100 Love Sonnets*. It's still my favorite collection of poems.

I do not love you as if you were salt-rose, or topaz,
or the arrow of carnations the fire shoots off.
I love you as certain dark things are to be loved,
in secret, between the shadow and the soul.

I love you as the plant that never blooms
but carries in itself the light of hidden flowers;
thanks to your love a certain solid fragrance,
risen from the earth, lives darkly in my body.

I love you without knowing how, or when, or from where,
I love you straightforwardly, without complexities or pride;
so I love you because I know no other way

than this: where I does not exist, nor you,
so close that your hand on my chest is my hand,
so close that your eyes close as I fall asleep.

CAROL Thursday, March 14

I'm starting to notice the skin in the bend of my elbow is getting loose and wrinkled. It's loosing the tautness all the beautiful young women still have. Bitches.

MAGGIE March 15

Waiting for these stupid letters is worse than filling out the applications. It's been 2 months. Louise already heard from Skidmore. Shit. When will I hear? Maybe I should have done early acceptance.

CAROL Tuesday, March 19

My cousin Carl emailed me. Uncle Chet is actually walking again, but they found cancer in Aunt El's lungs. A slow-growing kind. One she's probably had for ten years. She still can't eat much and is losing weight fast. I need a hug. Maggie is getting sick of me asking.

MAGGIE March 19

Mom is *so* needy. I can't stand her hovering.

chapter ten

_____

A Ghost to Her

MAGGIE March 28

Is school over yet? I'm starting to see the wisdom in dropping out. Every single day I have Alice Cooper's "School's Out" playing on repeat in my head. I think I'm going to go insane before this year ends. Am I done yet? When will I hear from the colleges? Ack!!

CAROL Saturday, March 30

Friends of Pennie's invited me to a salon at their home tonight. It was mostly musicians who performed, but they asked me to read some poetry. I read from my divorce collection.

Walking through
the cornfield   7am
catching dew on the tips
of ~~my~~ shoes   my bluish
eyes   guzzle   the rouge
chartreuse of spring   as
the check check of the
red-wing   punctuates the air.

Like a flicker   his flaming
new jeep   flies by
my daughter's face   ~~gazes~~
gazing out the window
contemplating a late pass.
She doesn't see me
wave   I am a ghost to her
these days.

I miss her already.

MAGGIE   April 2

Chris is such a moron. I could kill him. What the hell is he thinking, dropping out of school? He's not thinking. He's too doped up on 'E' to be able to think. Moron. He said he's planning on getting his GED, but everyone knows that's crap. He's done. It kills me that he's throwing so much away. Like going to film school. He was going to be the next Kevin Smith. He definitely has the talent. But no... Moron.

CAROL   Wednesday, April 3

Had a bad feeling when I saw that envelope today. My heart is breaking for Maggie.

MAGGIE   April 3

I knew I wouldn't get into every school I applied to, but did this one have to come first? Rejection is not fun. Why the hell don't they want me? What... am I not good enough for them? Well, screw them. BC sucks!

CAROL   Thursday, April 4

Sui and Phil came for Maggie's last concert. I was not able to hold back the tears. So what else is new?

Egad. This year is a string of lasts.

MAGGIE April 4

My last concert tonight. Aunt Susie and Uncle Phil came, which was really nice. Now that I think of it, they've come to all my concerts. And plays too. Wow. I can't believe they did that!

We did ok, but it's hard to get worked up about it after yesterday's news. At least Jack and I did well on our duet. "A Whole New World." It was difficult getting into it with that rejection on my mind. Got a bad case of rejection blues.

CAROL Monday, April 8

Two more envelopes arrived today. I can tell by their size it's not good news. I wish she hadn't applied to so many schools.

MAGGIE April 8

Vassar and Skidmore don't want me. God, I hate this. What did I do wrong?

MAGGIE April 9

Untitled (4)

twirling shadows.
how does one answer to such a question.
sweet platitudes, or a dagger of truth.
the pain makes it real.
reality is what is made, not what is thought.
the darkness does not hide,
but disguises what you do not wish to see when you look.
you still do not see.
there is no hope for you now.
was there ever?
the shadows know.
and they do not pause to answer,
no matter how much you beg.
do not lower yourself to such things.
there is no purpose when there is no hope.
there is just a black hole.
fill the void.

MAGGIE April 11

Yay. I got accepted to college. UMass wants me. In their theater arts department. UMass rocks. It's so close to home, though. Only 45 mins away. I really
don't want to stay around here. I don't want to be one of those people who
gets stuck in their home town for the rest of their lives. I still have two more
schools to hear from. I just want to escape. It's too small here.

CAROL Sunday, April 14

I spent the weekend on Long Island with Len. After a night of lovemaking,
we went to the beach, looking for treasures. Found some sea glass for my collection. He showed me where he fishes in the evenings. We talked about doing
a cookbook together. Am I crazy or what? Scares the daylights out of me.

I get to the ferry at ~~20~~ twenty past four
drop coins in the phone slot   to savor
your sonorous tones   before boarding the
John H.   for home.   I settle into an upper
deck spot   and watch a ~~curly~~ wavy haired
woman   backpack over her shoulder
climb steep steps   toting a brown bag
with violin case   bulging   like a fresh baked
baguette.   Leaning over the railing   her eyes
bite into a pony-tailed man   hair   white as
sea foam   returning to his car   while ~~her~~ heart
strings pluck a fervent ballad   and as her
lover opens his door   he glances up and
waves   her desire trembling in the salty air
and as he drives away   she stands   frozen
in place   until his long ~~tan~~ bronzed arm
reaches   out the window   ~~one~~
one last time.

I see you lying in bed   spent   from our
weekend rendezvous   humming a tune

you gently fiddle with   as the fog horn
wails a lamentation   and the ferry
slowly pulls out of its slip
into the soothing sound.

MAGGIE   April 16

Well, BU and Mt. Holyoke are added to the list. *sigh* It looks like I'll be going to UMass. Dad is wicked happy. At least all the waiting's over. I wonder what dorm they'll put me in. It's weird thinking about living away from home. I don't even remember what the UMass campus looks like. I haven't been there since sixth grade, when Dad took me to a basketball game. I didn't bother to take a tour, because I was so sure I wasn't gonna go there. Guess I was wrong.

CAROL   Wednesday, April 17

Talked to Ruth today. Rose got into all the schools she applied to. She's going to Skidmore. It was painful to hear about. Can't believe how envious I feel. Why couldn't I just be happy for her? I can't help thinking I went wrong somewhere.

MAGGIE   April 18

Natasha and Chris came over today to work on Nat's and my catapult for Physics. Well, Nat came to work; Chris came because he needed a ride. But while driving to Southampton, Chris was insisting that ecstasy doesn't kill your brain cells. Nat and I were like, "Yeah Chris, it really does." I can't believe he didn't know that. Oh wait, he probably didn't know that 'cause his brain cells have already been killed by ecstasy. The ultimate Catch-22.

MAGGIE   April 22

Well, we're all going to college. Me and my friends. Yay! Louise is going to Skidmore, Jeanne—WPI, Carrie—Ithaca, Beth—Bridgewater State, Dave—Western New England, and of course, Ann and Nat are going to UMass with me. Ann's gonna be living on campus too. Nat's gonna live at home and commute. I don't know why she'd ever want to do that. Ann's talking about rooming together. I'm not sure I want us to be roommates. Afraid it might mess up our friendship. What will I do without my friends next year?

CAROL Saturday, April 27

I started estrogen today. I'm pausing *The Pause*. I can't stand the hot flashes anymore. I'll try anything for a decent night's sleep.

CAROL Wednesday, May 1

Oh cripes. Maggie is going to Florida tomorrow with a group of her classmates. I'm a wreck about her flying. About her getting sunburned. About her eating enough. If I'm like this for *this* trip, what will I be like when she goes to Europe? I don't even want to go there.

MAGGIE May 4

Woot! Disney baby! I love being a senior. I mean getting to take two days off from school to go to Disney World with my class. Where's the downside of that? Actually, the downside seems to be the mongo sunburn I'm sporting now. The one I got at the water park. But this trip rocks. Went to Epcot, MGM Studios, Downtown Disney, Typhoon Lagoon, Magic Kingdom and Pleasure Island. All in three days.

CAROL Sunday, May 5

Turned the soil in my vegetable garden today.

MAGGIE May 6

The main purpose of Grad Night is the actual Grad Night Party at the Magic Kingdom. An all night party with tons of other schools. Big fun. Only one problem. We missed it! Our liaison with Disney told us it was on Saturday night. Well...turns out it was on Friday. So while we were shopping at downtown Disney, thousands of seniors were partying it up in Cinderella's castle. Bah!

We went back to Downtown Disney to go to Pleasure Island. That definitely wasn't something we were planning to do on this trip. Club hopping. But we did. At least most of us did. I couldn't get Ann or Misty to go into any of the clubs. I don't know what was up with them. They were such buzz kills. I ended up grinding with this random cute guy who didn't believe I was still in high school. Must have been the backless top!

CAROL   Monday, May 6

She's back in one piece with very little sunburn and most of her body-weight still intact. Praise be.

MAGGIE   May 9

Think I'll make Mom a CD for Mother's Day. With some of our favorite songs. "For Baby," Peter, Paul and Mary; "My Girl," Temptations; "Maggie May," Rod Stewart; "Baby Mine," from Dumbo; "I'll Stand By You," Pretenders; "In My Life," Judy Collins; "Seasons of Love," from Rent; "Angel," Sarah McLachlan; "Colorblind," Counting Crows; "Lucky," Bif Naked; "Do What You Have To Do," Sarah McLachlan; "Wild Horses," The Sundays; "I'll Remember You," Sophie Zelmani; "Full of Grace," Sarah McLachlan; "Imagine," John Lennon; "Part of Your World," from Little Mermaid; "Stand By Me," Ben. E. King; "Storybook Love," Willy DeVille; "Time of Your Life," Green Day; and "Forever Young," Pretenders.

Of course, Mom will cry when she plays it.

MAGGIE   May 15

Senior skip day. A time-honored tradition. And I almost missed it. 'Cause I skipped the day before. Had I checked my email, I would have seen that Louise wrote to me about it, but didn't read my email and went to school. I got there and no one was in the hallway. By the time the warning bell rang, a dozen people showed up. I finally got what was going on, genius that I am, and booked it to the nurse's office. Mrs. M. was nice enough to send me home, since I was feeling so sick, cough, cough. Yeah. I'm wicked sick. Sick of school. I just hope Giordano doesn't kick our butts for skipping. Aah!

MAGGIE   May 16

Mom and I went to see *Cabaret* at Symphony Hall. I liked the production, but Mom didn't so much. She's critical 'cause she played Sally Bowles when she was young. Which actually rocks. Mom as Sally Bowles. Can't really picture it, but I guess it's pretty awesome.

I did something today that I've hardly ever done. Pulled the divorced-kid switcheroo. Since Mom and I were seeing *Cabaret*, I asked Dad to go to the Europe meeting for us. Only thing is, permission slips were being signed at this meeting to allow anyone under 18 to drink while we're over there. Of course, I didn't mention to Mom that's what the meeting was about. Whoops. And since Dad doesn't have a problem w/me drinking... Just want to have the option.

CAROL Saturday, May 18

Today was Belle's birthday party. And though we've had our ups and downs, she's a dear friend. I'm glad we were able to patch things up. I made a platter of asparagus marinated with balsamic and garlic vinaigrette to bring. Garnished with roasted red peppers. Belle put on some great CD's and all us girls danced up a storm. Had lots of fun. Just what I needed.

CAROL Monday, May 20

The grief I feel about Maggie and Aunt El is intense. So I called Len. Sometimes it's good, sometimes not. Today it was delicious. He said all the right things.

MAGGIE May 21

We had senior solos tonight. I sang "Across the Universe." I love the song, but only rehearsed it twice. Play practice for *Murder by the Book* has eaten up the last two weeks. I'm so exhausted. I sounded like crap. Not the note I wanted to end on, no pun intended.

Dave played the theme from *The Godfather* on his trumpet. He was great. But Nat, she was the star of the evening. She sang "Stormy Weather" and it was the best I've ever heard her sing. Everyone in the place went nuts. We ended the night singing "Graduation (Friends Forever)." Which of course, made everyone cry. I can't believe the end is almost here.

MAGGIE May 23

This play is a joke. What a way to go out of drama. W/the crappiest play of all time. *Murder By the Book.* Ugh. And to think, if it weren't for the construction on the auditorium, I could be staring in the *Three Penny Opera.* Instead, we're doing dinner theater in the cafeteria. And tonight's performance cemented the joke that is this play. In one scene, during the second act, everyone on stage froze. I was backstage, so I couldn't do anything about it. Everyone forgot their lines. Tony tried to fake it, but ended up having to rush offstage 'cause he was laughing so hard. A mess. A hilarious mess, but still a mess.

It just seems unfair that this is the play I got stuck with. Everyone else who's in it has already been in another play this year. At least I got to stage-manage *Ring Around the Moon*, so I had some valuable theater work, but as far as acting goes, this is it. My big finale. If only I graduated last year. Then I would have stared in *Midsummer*... *Sigh*

CAROL Thursday, May 23

I will miss all these people next year. All Maggie's friends and their moms. What will I be without them? I don't know how to do all this letting go.

MAGGIE May 26

I think everyone in their lifetime should go swimming at midnight at least once. That's what Natasha, Louise, Jeanne, Carrie and I did last night. We drove out to Chesterfield and went swimming in the river. It was so much fun. The only light was from the moon, and we were in the middle of the woods. Kinda scary, but it also added to the excitement. Jeanne wasn't too happy w/ me when I started humming the theme from Jaws. I swear I felt something brush against my leg.

MAGGIE May 27

Hmmm. I really ought to be studying for finals. I ought to, but won't. 'Cause I'm gonna graduate no matter what grades I get, so who cares!! It's senioritis, baby!

CAROL Wednesday, May 29

I had dinner with Sue Teece, aka Lucy. She calls me Ethel. It seemed fitting to meet up with her, as she was one of Mag's 4th grade teachers. I still miss seeing her and Leslie everyday. Gosh, it's been three years since I left the Norris School Library. Can't wait to read *When The Cows Got Loose* to her class. God only knows when that will happen.

MAGGIE June 3

Senior week. The best idea ever. What better way to spend the week of graduation than with your classmates doing chill stuff? Today we went to High Meadows. Seniors from all over Western Mass were there. Louise and I spent an hour and a half by the pool just sunbathing. And while all the loser lower classmen were in class, HA, we played mini-golf, ate burgers, sang karaoke and hung out with hundreds of people. Two of them being Waren and Kayla. Turns out Westfield High was there too. Kayla tried to tie-dye her jeans. Didn't work too well. This was the first time I'd seen Waren since he came out. He seems much more relaxed and happy now.

CAROL Tuesday, June 4

Saw Renee today. Cried for most of my session with her.

MAGGIE June 4

Tonight was senior banquet. We got all dressed up only to spend a couple hours waiting around for our yearbooks. But at least it gave me a chance to have most people sign it.

Mrs. Leep showed this video montage of our years at HRHS. She included clips from our class trips and pictures of all of us. I have to remember to buy a copy from her. Some wicked funny pictures of the guys in my class. He-he. Blackmail material.

MAGGIE June 6

Senior breakfast was this morning, at the Westhampton Church. Jeanne, Kailey and I drove up together. It would have been nice, if it weren't for the fact I felt wicked sick through the whole thing. I couldn't eat a single pancake w/o feeling like I'd hurl. Guess it's just the stress from tomorrow. At least I relaxed enough for graduation rehearsal at Smith. Which took FOR-E-VER. Who knew it was so difficult to get everyone in alphabetical order. I think we may all be stupid.

CAROL Saturday, June 8

You come for her graduation
the daughter I conceived with
your old friend   which needless
less to say   complicates things.
I become unhinged as we leave
the house   my dither displacing
itself into a broken cameras   that
I cart to this noteworthy affair.
I could only do this with you
he who tenderly held my hand
through my deflowering ceremony
who picked the petals of my maiden
hood   snatching up the part of me
that awaiting to be plucked.

Standing beside you   as I watch
my daughter accept her diploma
romping like a child into this
dubious world of adulthood
I can't help but wonder
if she will someday be
as lucky as me.

Sui and Phil also came down from Woodstock. The ceremony was beautiful.
I held it together as much as I could. There were some awkward moments
afterwards when we all gathered in front of John M. Greene Hall. Of course,
Rickey and Teresa were there. Her resentment of me was so obvious. I want
her to like me. For Maggie's sake. But it's not gonna happen in this lifetime.
Oh well. Just glad Len was with me.

MAGGIE June 8

Wow! I'm a high school graduate! I haven't slept in 24 hours! I partied all night at the New England Health and Racquet Club! I swam! I laughed! I played Wolleyball! This is awesome!

CAROL Sunday, June 9

After you leave   I plant ~~the~~ leeks
tenderly troweling a trench

positioning each pencil-like
plant   pressing their rootlets

into fertile loam   giving focus
to the longing   that lingers

on the back of my tongue.
It's harder to say goodbye

the cultivation done on this
relationship   reaping a fine

harvest ~~much~~ sooner than
expected   a profusion

of growth   far exceeding
estimated forecasts   and as ~~I~~

I place the last sprout in the
sandy soil   my tears are the

first spatter of water   these
allium babies will receive.

MAGGIE June 13

It's so weird doing things that have been tradition for so long, for the last time. Like Debbie's parties. The best way to celebrate the end of school. We usually hang out, eat food, swim, and play on her rope swing. This year was so different. Spent the entire three hours signing yearbooks. Well, that and eating food. Lots of cake. Of course, it made it even weirder 'cause I've already graduated. At least I'll be able to see Debbie whenever I want. I'm so glad she also works at the UMass library. One more familiar face.

CAROL Saturday, June 15

Pennie helped me throw a party for Maggie and her friends. We spent two days preparing the food. A throwback to the days we worked in restaurants together. Four girls showed up. We had enough chow for a friggin' army. I can't figure out what went wrong. Probably the 'no booze' rule. It was fine with me, but I felt really bad for Maggie.

MAGGIE June 16

What happened to all my other friends? Nat, Louise, Carrie, Jeanne, Dave, Shawn, Jack, Chris. I just got ditched by almost everyone I knew. What the hell?! Why didn't you guys come to my party?

CAROL Monday, June 17

Looks like Ard Hoyt will be the one illustrating *When the Cows Got Loose*. I have to call Leslie. She'll be thrilled. Kevin sent some samples of his work. He has a great sense of whimsy. His cows are adorable. I wonder how he'll depict Ida Mae. I've had her pictured in my head for so many years. Hope he comes close.

MAGGIE June 18

Got a package in the mail from Lizzie and Sue. A graduation gift. It was so sweet of them. A big ass towel with my name on it, a wash cloth to match, a few bars of soap, and a hand mitt with little dragon, knight, wizard, king and queen characters on the fingers. It's so cute. I'm all set for college now. Not really…

I can't believe I'm leaving in two months. I miss everything already. My house, my room, my friends. My parents. Everything.

CAROL Thursday, June 20

We sold the trampoline.

It's gone   that vestige of my
daughter's youth   strapped to the
back of a pickup and ripped away   now
sprawling recklessly in a neighbor's back
yard.   Little did they know   ~~that~~ late last
night   I seized one final frolic   climbed aboard
the rusty relic that lazed for years on my front lawn
and before I knew what happened   my nighty took
flight.   I whipped that baby off my menopausal body
and bounced   naked as a newborn   on that tarnished
trampoline   soaring like the titmouse that nests in my
porch   while a lecherous moon   leered   through limbs
of lanky oaks   surely amused   by this midnight trollop.

I watched my neighbors grapple with it the next day
cart it across the grass   reckoning how in the heck
they'd get it home   while I sat   and smirked
knowing full well   how I had romped
with this ol' codger   the night before.

MAGGIE June 20

"These are the times that try men's souls." Paine was only trying to fight a revolution. Me, I've got a much larger struggle. College. The enormity of the situation is just starting to hit me.

I mean, it was bad enough having to say good-bye to all those people from HRHS. Some of them I've known since kindergarten. Jeanne, and Corinne, and Kris, and Cecilia. I have such a clear picture in my mind of us playing around the giant roots of the maple trees at school. They formed this big bowl shape, and we'd fill them w/leaves and hide in them. And Brien, Waren and I used to plot about digging up the treasure we were convinced was buried under a boulder behind the swing set.

Now all going off in different directions. I knew I was in trouble when

Vitamin C's "Graduation" made me cry. Nostalgia is already creeping up. We haven't even been out of school a month. But now, orientation is in a couple of days. It's my first step into the craziness of UMass.

I can't believe I'm going to 'ZooMass.' I've been so adamant about not going there, and now look where I am. Isn't it ironic? Sing it, Alanis.

chapter eleven

At Least I'll Die High

CAROL Friday, June 21

I had lunch with Joanie. I am beside myself with grief about Maggie. But mostly about Aunt El. I need to say goodbye to her and don't know how. I really want a drink. Joan suggested I write a letter. Pennie and Belle did too.

The plant you gave me shares a shelf in my bedroom with a pink begonia. They sit quietly beside the window, soaking up sunlight, at the foot of my bed. It's in bloom now; those orangey/yellow blossoms, like dolphins leaping from the sea, remind me of you. I will transplant it soon, to a bigger pot, where I will tend to it so that it grows strong and continues to flourish....

A start, at least.

MAGGIE June 25

I'm so exhausted. The longest three days ever. Didn't think orientation would be this much work. I had to learn the campus all over again. Hadn't been there since grade school, to see a game at the Mullins Center.

We took a tour on Saturday and saw the dorms. Sylvan is too far away from the main part of campus, Southwest is too crazy, and Northeast has rooms like prison cells [slept there this weekend]. So Central is my first choice. They have bigger rooms, and it's closest to campus.

I had my UCard picture taken and registered for classes. My temporary advisor showed me how to work the registration system, which is by phone. Kinda messed up. But I'm signed up for Beginning Techniques in Performance, Play Analysis, Biology of Cancer and AIDS, Calculus for Life and Society, and Performance Management. Thirteen credits. I should take fifteen, but I couldn't find another class to fit in. Oh well. I'll make it up later.

CAROL Tuesday, June 25

Rickey picked me up and drove us to UMass for the last part of orientation. He told me how sad he's feeling. We talked about his freshman year in college, when his parents split up. How they dropped him off in September and by the time he came home for Thanksgiving, they were separated. Without breathing a word to him. Was our marriage doomed from the start?

We had lunch with Maggie and Ann, then toured the campus ourselves. I saw it through new eyes, now that Maggie's enrolled here. More beautiful than I remembered. Rickey and I felt like a team again. His relief about the cost of this college helps. We're the only ones who can go through this initiation with her.

CAROL Saturday, June 29

I have been running errands for the last four days. Picking up travelers checks, an umbrella, money belt, camera, film, socks, yada, yada, yada. I went to three different WalMarts to get the damn money belt. I'm her servant right now. It keeps things smooth between us. I have surrendered to the moment. Who will hold me together when she leaves on Monday?

MAGGIE June 30

Oh god. I'm going to Europe tomorrow. Aah! And I'm supposed to sleep now? Ha! What if the plane explodes over the Atlantic? At least I'll die high.

CAROL Monday, July 1

I just dropped Maggie at the Fire Station. I'm trying to hold it together. Sending her to Florida was one thing. Two months from now it's college. I need to buy more Kleenex.

MAGGIE July 2

I'm sitting in Heathrow Airport. That's right, baby, I'm in London!! Waiting for the flight to Paris. Ooh, our flight was just called. Ah oui, c'est Paris!

CAROL Tuesday, July 2

I'm at Sui and Phil's for the 4th. Johnny's coming for a couple days. He'll make me laugh. Help take my mind off Maggie. Please! Just keep her away from lechers and booze!

MAGGIE July 4

I don't think there's anything more amazing than strolling on the streets of Paris and just breathing in the city. Its beauty and age are humbling. Back in the states, we think it's amazing when a building from the 18th century still stands. That's a year in the history of Paris. We are so small in the world.

Walking through the gardens of Versailles, I couldn't stop thinking how Kings have walked the same paths. We saw Louis XVI's bed. His bed!! It was a tiny bed, at that.

Notre Dame is incredible. The flying buttresses, the gargoyles...its gothic architecture, all so beautiful. It was so dark inside, yet you look at the rose and other stained glass windows and you are overwhelmed by color and light.

I heard a baby babbling in French on the metro tonight. It was something I never thought about. A baby learning to talk. But in French, not English. That experience alone convinced me making English our national language would be a mistake.

Last night, I had my first glass of wine. Sitting in the restaurant, sipping wine, I never felt more part of the world. Despite everyone speaking a language I have only a passable grasp of. It just felt right. Like I belonged there.

Tomorrow we leave the city for Biarritz. Then Spain. I hope I don't lose this feeling.

CAROL Friday, July 5

I'm plaguing everyone with maps and itinerary. What time is it? They're at the Eiffel Tower now. Oh my gosh. That means they're in Versailles. Look, here it is, on the map!!

They're on the TGV to Biarritz today. I'm boring myself with this stuff. Wishing I were there. I wanted to stow away in her backpack, but she claimed I wouldn't fit. Fat chance, Mom!! The noive!!

MAGGIE July 5

The Atlantic is freezing here. First thing Ann and I did after we all checked into the hotel was head down to the water. Lasted for a whole 10 seconds. Wicked cold. Then it started raining, so we went back to the hotel. The beach was so cool, though. A bunch of those old-fashioned striped changing tents lined the sand. I'd never seen them before.

After dinner, Mrs. Hill took a bunch of us on a tour of the town. I took pictures of some stunning hydrangea bushes. They were so blue. And I got some yummy pistachio ice cream.

MAGGIE July 6

We crossed the border into Spain. I kept noticing all these people in cars wearing white T-shirts with red scarves around their necks. Then it hit me. This week is the Running of the Bulls. We were close to Pamplona. And a couple of those people will probably get seriously injured.

Our first stop was Bilbao. To visit the new Guggenheim—the weirdest looking building. Supposed to resemble ships, but looks more like a bunch of metal waves.

Tonight we're staying outside Burgos. So today we explored the town. I saw my first red pigeon. Rick, Jack, Tara, Ann and I wandered around, looking for a place to buy ice cream.

I plotted with Tara, Jack and Cindy to sneak out of the hotel. Tara's window comes out, so we went up on the roof. Ann was being all not fun and wouldn't come. She actually went to sleep at 9:00!!

CAROL Monday, July 8

Holy Toledo! I just got off the phone with Maggie. She's alive and in Madrid. I think I feel the house sighing.

MAGGIE July 9

Madrid is an awesome city. Spent the past two days exploring it. I stood in the exact center of Spain. We went to the Prado Museum and saw the great Spanish artists. Goya, El Greco, Velazquez. Then we went to the Reina Sofia Gallery. And there it was. *Guernica*. The most moving piece I've ever seen. The terror expressed in it is palpable. It's violent without being offensive, in large part because it's without color. Shades of gray, in more ways than one.

It took us forever to find it, but we also saw the statue of Cervantes and Don Quixote. Such an infamous literary character. I've always loved that book. And "tilting at windmills" is one of my favorite expressions—we all do it. Sitting on the base of the statue, I was struck by the rush of cultural experiences I've had in the last week. I mean, I've gone from Rodin sculptures, to the Gardens of Versailles, to Salvador Dali's *El gran masturbador*. And the trip's not even over. I've seen more this week than some people will see in their entire lifetimes. I am so lucky.

Today we went to Toledo. Now I understand the necessity of daily siestas. Spanish afternoons are scorching. At least I got some kick jewelry. Toledo's known for their black jewelry and swords. Weird. Jack got three swords. Getting them on the plane should be interesting.

CAROL Tuesday, July 9

I wonder how she's doing. Is she safe? Hope she isn't too homesick. Can't wait to see my baby-girl.

MAGGIE July 10

Spain has been good to me. Except for the hangover.

CAROL Wednesday, July 10

Rickey and I picked Maggie up at the Fire Station. Waited in his car for an hour or so reminiscing about our trip to Europe. Before she was born. Our favorite spot in France was Épernay. The first town we settled in after leaving Paris in our Citroën.

We laughed about traversing the Alps, on the fringe of avalanche season, with boulders aiming to block the road. Only to find out, when we reached the top, the snow plow was still trying to get through. We totally freaked out and about-faced our little car, to journey down the mountain again. We were so in love back then. Wonder if he ever thinks about it like I do. What ever happened to us?

It's so good to see Maggie. I just spent an hour on her bed hearing about her adventures. This trip has changed her. She told me she drank some wine while she was there. "Are you mad, Mom?" I tried to stay cool. It's not how I'm feeling inside. How could they let all these underage kids drink without their parent's consent?

That wasn't the case. Rickey signed a permission form before she left. I'll ring his…now breathe, Carol, 1, 2, 3….

MAGGIE July 15

I got my dorm assignment and Mom is freaking out. I'm in one of the towers. JQA to be exact. In the heart of party central, on the 14th floor. I'll be rooming with a sophomore named Jade Petterson. Mom keeps bugging me to call her. I hope she's half-way decent and likes *Alias*.

CAROL Monday, July 15

Of all the dorms on UMass campus, Maggie gets JQA. If I could pick any dorm I'd hate to have her live in, this would be the one. They say you get what you fear. Shit. This is it, baby. Sending my girl to that jungle. If one of those upperclassman lays a hand on her, I'll have their eyes plucked out with needle-nose pliers and their dicks super-glued to their navels.

MAGGIE July 18

I called Jade and left a message with her brother. He said she was at work. He sounded pretty cool. I guess.

CAROL Sunday, July 21

Another weekend with Len. He played the piano for me. A piece he wrote, plus "Fur Elise," which always makes me melt. We went to the beach. Collected some shells. Swam in the ocean. Cooked dinner together. Spent the rest of the time in his loft. I'm a new woman. YES!

CAROL Monday, July 22

I went to the President's reception at Smith with Pennie. To welcome Carol Christ. The new chancellor. The food was fabulous. Smith knows how to lay out a feast. Pennie has taken me to the faculty club a few times this year. One night we had our own a private dining room. I felt like a queen. Pennie really spoils me and it feels good to me right now. Helps alleviate the sadness that's governing my heart.

MAGGIE July 22

I still haven't heard from my roommate. I wish Ann and I were in the same dorm. She's on the other side of campus. In Sylvan. On the fifth floor of McNamara. Too far away.

CAROL Tuesday, July 23

It was 10:30. On a hot summer night. I couldn't wait to dive into bed in my air-conditioned room. Leaning against the sink, I smeared cucumber cleanser on exhausted cheeks. Suddenly, I noticed something fluttering near my shoulder. Assuming it was a moth, I continued to slather. Turns out, it wasn't a moth. It was a bird. An honest-to-God feathered creature soaring around my bathroom. I screamed, a loud, bloodcurdling scream and raced down the hall to fetch Maggie. Bursting into her room, my heart thumped faster than my chest could endure. I jabbered incoherently about seagulls in the bathroom. Alfred Hitchcock directed the scene, as Maggie sat at her computer, rolling her eyes.

I grabbed her by the arm and dragged her down the hall. We made it to the staircase. The bird skimmed our heads. We screamed, then grabbed towels from the railing and hit the deck. Our bodies trembled beneath the terry-cloth shields. "Mom," she wailed. "What should we do?" I gulped, sensing I hadn't a clue.

I crawled into my bedroom, only yards away, signaling Maggie to follow. The bird kept swooping as we scrambled into the room. Hopping on the bed, we sat and shook. I lifted the receiver to my ear. To call Neal. *Ztztztztztz* is what I heard. Maggie forgot to sign offline. My adrenals went into overload. You'd think Godzilla was on the other side of the door.

It was obvious we weren't going to be rescued. My feet dangled over the floor. I was afraid to touch it. There may be rats under the bed. My mind was a garbage dump. I took some deep breaths. "We need to arm ourselves," I said.

I went to my closet. Climbed into the heaviest pair of jeans I own. Put on thick socks and combat boots. Said a prayer. I pictured the President slipping the Medal of Honor around my neck. Maggie zipped up her sweatshirt and pulled on the hood, tying the string tight to her chin. I threw a towel over my head, clutching it to my throat. We tiptoed to the door. My stomach lurched to my mouth. I looked at Maggie and froze. "I thought you were a feminist," she sniveled.

"I hope I'm alive when you go through menopause," I said.

I cracked the door and peeked out. *SWOOSH*. The bird whizzed by. I slammed the door shut, shoving my back against it, picturing a massive swarm of gulls on the other side.

"Some feminist," she said. I inched open the door. *SWOOSH. Swoosh. Swoosh.*

"Mom, what if it has a heart attack?" Yeah, well, what about me, I wanted to say. "Just get me back to my room," she pleaded. I grabbed a stick that was out of work due to the air-conditioning, typically used to prop up a window. Now drafted for battle.

I cracked the door again. No flapping in sight. I opened it a little wider. With stick in hand and towels to toss on the terrified creature, we stepped into the hallway. I peered both ways, then dashed down the hall, my daughter hustling behind. I got her to her room. We slammed the door and leaned our backs against it. We slid down onto the floor, exhausted from the menacing event, eventually rolling into a fit of laughter.

MAGGIE July 24

Somewhere in this house is a bird that's freaking out. I'm afraid to go out of my room. Well, I guess I won't be going to college after all.

CAROL Thursday, July 25

We haven't seen the bird again. Don't know how it got in or out of the house. But every time I think of it, I look over my shoulder and get ready to duck.

CAROL Monday, July 29

We just got back from Culver's Lake to see Ma. This trip to New Jersey is always so beautiful this time of year. Loosestrife abounds in every hollow along interstate 84. I like riding in the car with Maggie. We can drive for hours and say little to each other. It's perfectly okay. She is the only person I can do that with. She is my Hanging Gardens. My Great Wall. My Taj Mahal. She is my home.

This visit, we brought Ma down to the lake for a swim. She is old and wobbly and needs our help to walk. We hooked arms and ambled along the lake road. Of course, getting her in and out of the water was a stitch. Ma has a gift of laughing at herself.

Our time with her was delicious. We sat on the sofa for a movie, the three of us cuddling close, eating popcorn, like in a theater. Our hearts are so wide now, with Maggie's going to college so near. I am a novel between these bookends of mine. How will my spine hold up when they are gone?

MAGGIE July 29

Ma was so sweet. She's the only person I know who gets excited about braces. I'm so glad I could do that for her.

CAROL Wednesday, July 31

Got a postcard from Greg. He's almost done. Can't begin to fathom "DIVORCE PAPERS" released in the midst of all this sadness.

MAGGIE August 2

Mom's going to see Aunt El tomorrow. She wants me to go. I just can't do that right now. Too much to deal with. I'd just go there and feel sad and helpless. Have to focus on getting ready for school. I'm getting nervous. Need to make a list. I still have all my shopping and packing. Ack! Nothing else can be on my plate right now. I gave Mom a teddy bear to bring to Aunt El. I just hope it's enough. It has to be.

CAROL Saturday, August 3

Pennie drove me to the Cape. To hold me up for this visit. I was anxious at the prospect of seeing Aunt El. She's waiting to die. I prayed to say the right thing.

She was sitting on the sofa when I arrived. A wisp of who she was. I tried to act normal as I handed her the Victoria Secret bag stuffed with the teddy bear from Maggie. She snuggled it to her chin. This was not normal at all. Her jewelry was spread across the dinner table. She had something she wanted to give me. Both of us knew why I was really here. I went along with it anyway.

She handed me a bracelet. The biggest I've ever seen. Bands of sterling circled in turquoise beads. Shaped like tears. I clasped it to my wrist. I wanted to run and hide. This does not belong to me. Tears surged as I glanced at her. I bargained in my head. If I don't take the bracelet, will you spare her life?

We sat and said little. I told her of Maggie's escapades this summer. Everything sounded so lame. The urgency of each word filled the room. Uncle Chet hovered. "Oh Chet, stop it," she said. He is also at a loss. How will he let go of the love of his life? Stumbling like a colt, I'm sure.

CAROL Sunday, August 11

Maggie and I spent the last three days at Sui and Phil's. Matt and Becky are up from Panama. Andrew was there too. It's so rare we get to see them together like this. Mag and I stayed in the RV. Our last day we planned a picnic. I brought food for our celebration. Plus a cake for Maggie's birthday and college send-off. But she broke down last night. Couldn't stop crying. Begged me to take her home. I was really upset because I needed to be with my family. I'm feeling so sad myself and being with them helps. She begged and begged. I had to give in. Then whined and complained the whole way home. I am a bad mother.

MAGGIE August 11

Mom's still mad at me. For asking to leave Aunt Susie's. I just couldn't stay there. I'm feeling too sad. I needed to be home in my own room. I wish she'd understand. It was like premature homesickness. I just started imagining how I might feel at school, and it overwhelmed me. The only thing I could think of that would help was being back home. You can't feel homesick for a place you're at.

CAROL Tuesday, August 13

We went to Linens n' Things and spent $150 on her college stuff. Two sets of sheets, a bunch of pillow cases, a fleecy blanket, a quilt, an egg crate, a shower tote, plastic container to store stuff in, a head towel, a laundry basket and hangers. We got it all. 'Cause my baby's going to college.

MAGGIE August 14

Got all this stuff for college. Now I have to pack my things. I'm not sure what to take. I feel dizzy just thinking about it.

CAROL Sunday, August 18

Another weekend on Long Island with Len. He's an oasis for me right now. I am grateful for the solace he gives me. And I think his heart is finally opening up to me.

I whimper these days   when I
leave her room   weep as
I walk   down the hall
crossing off the hours till
she's gone.   Starts college
in a week   drafting her

own narrative   as I
straddle the sidebar of
my life story   wondering
what comes next   when
this chapter as mother
is through.

MAGGIE August 23

My stuff is all over the house. Everywhere I turn there are piles of confusion. Where did it all come from? I don't think we'll get it into Dad's car. Oh my god, I'm actually going to college. And I haven't even talked to my roommate yet.

CAROL Sunday, August 25

Belle and I met in Ashfield to see Marcia sing. She went to music camp this summer and her group is on tour. I'm trying to stay busy so I don't have to feel. The music was joyful and moving. Belle and I could not get over how beautiful Marcia is. Her spirit illuminated the church.

We got invited to a dinner party after the concert. The home was like a museum. The furniture—all works of art. I felt so alone in this crowd of people. Staying busy is not working very well. Sometimes I can hardly breathe from the pain I feel. Wherever I am, I only want to cry.

CAROL Monday, August 26

Greg called. He was in Southampton and had 25 copies of *DIVORCE PAPERS* to give me. He asked me to meet him at his mom's. The timing is providential.

The book is so exquisite, I couldn't speak. So I cried. Greg is an artist. Worth every morsel of frustration I experienced along the way. My gratitude is boundless. My respect for him is profound. All I could think about was Maggie. I couldn't wait to show her this.

MAGGIE August 26

Oh god. I leave in six days. I can't wait to get away from Mom. She's driving me crazy. Only six days. Shit.

CAROL Tuesday, August 27

Sara, our new librarian, left a message on my answering machine. "Hi Carol. Congratulations. We heard about *DIVORCE PAPERS* and would love to schedule a reading." News travels fast. I need to catch my breath. "Call me so we can set a date for September." Am I really ready for this?

MAGGIE August 27

I finally got to talk to my roommate. She sounds nice and all. She's from Lowell. Near where Aunt Judy used to live. This is going to be so weird. Rooming with someone I don't even know. I'm so used to not having to share anything. Pitfall of being an only child.

CAROL Wednesday, August 28

Maggie and I had dinner at Pennie and Kermit's. I brought one of my a chocolate mousse cakes that Pennie requested for the occasion. And a copy of *DIVORCE PAPERS* for her. Jean-Jacque, Marion and Perrine are here from Paris. They've been living in Tunisia for a few years and are visiting our country this month. Pennie acted as translator throughout the night. Maggie beamed as she spoke of her summer adventures in France. The best graduation gift I could have given to this blessed child of mine.

I gazed at Jean-Jacque and Marion. Perrine is their only child. I wondered how it will be when she goes off to college or leaves their Parisian nest. Will it hurt them as much as it's hurting me? Are the French exempt from this kind of pain? I could already see it in their eyes.

MAGGIE August 28

Mom and I had dinner at Pennie's. She had her friends from France visiting this summer. She wanted us to meet them. I got to speak some French with them. Not much, but un peu. They told us someday we should visit them in Paris. Awesome. Ah, Paris! How I miss thee!

CAROL Friday, August 30

I steal hugs and breathe in her essence whenever I can. Press lips to top of her silky head, hoping to impart the wisdom of the ancients, or at least something she'll need for that coed dorm, gulp, we move her into next week.

CAROL Saturday, August 31

Maggie, Rickey and I had dinner at Harvest Valley for her 18th birthday. We sat on the deck, high on Mt. Tom, where the view of the Pioneer Valley is exquisite. We swore we could see our old house on College Highway. The little Cape where I came to live with Rickey from Philadelphia. The night amazed me. There was no charge between us. Rickey and I are finally at peace. We are the only two people on this planet that feel the same way about Maggie.

After, we went back to our house for dessert. We ate the cake I brought back from Sui's. A sachertorte recipe from my baking days. My craving for chocolate is huge right now. I used up a half a roll of film taking shots of Rickey and Maggie on the sofa. He sat beside her—his arm wrapped around her shoulder the rest of the night. Holding on for dear life. Not quite ready to lose his little girl. It was sweet. The love in the air filled me with its goodness. So pure I could almost taste it. Maybe it was the chocolate….

MAGGIE August 31

Dad let Mom come with us to Harvest Valley, for our annual birthday dinner. It was kinda weird having her there. But good too. They acted okay with each other. No fights or anything. Dad gave me a cell phone. Yay! Mom's really glad. She was hoping he would do that. To give her peace of mind when I'm at UMass. Shit. That's tomorrow. I'm going to college tomorrow. I just hope I can sleep tonight.

CAROL Sunday, September 1, 9:30pm

Who am I kidding? She'll be fine. It's me I worry about.

I thought about jumping from her dorm window.

Ate chocolate instead.

After getting her settled in, as much as we could stand, we hung around for a while, until she was ready to have us leave. We watched her take off on her bike, to have dinner with Ann. As she blithely peddled down the driveway, her braids blowing in the breeze, I pictured her at different stages of her life, in awe of the young woman she's become. Then crumpled onto a stone wall in tears. Rickey gave me a hug. Our hearts were as wide as the day she was born.

After he dropped me off, the loneliness was gut wrenching. I hugged myself as I paced around the house. I went to her bedroom, but couldn't go in. I sat in the family room and felt its emptiness close in on me. I tried watching *Alias,* but nothing made sense. I wanted to call her, but thought I shouldn't. What's she doing now, fourteen stories up? With all that testosterone just down the hall! Does she like her roommate? I stared at the phone, willing it to ring. I got my wish, two hours later.

Maggie called in tears.

I wanted to drive up and get her.

I knew I couldn't.

I don't know how to do this!

How do I let her go?

MAGGIE September 1

Mom, Dad and I packed up my things, stuffed it into Dad's jeep, and drove to the University of Massachusetts in Amherst. My new home. I thought I was going to puke in the car. Or hyperventilate, at least. They moved me into one of the Towers. I can't believe I'm living in one of the party dorms in the center of ZooMass. I'm really not a big party girl.

Anyway, my parents helped me get my room set up, then left. My roommate had already moved in, but hadn't shown up yet. I was all alone my first night at college. Just me. Fourteen stories up. There's only two other freshmen on this whole floor—two guys who live in the other wing—so I had absolutely no one to talk to. My RA had a meeting w/the three of us, to lay out the ground rules. He doesn't care what we do, as long as he doesn't get in trouble. So it's okay to smoke pot, as long as you put a towel under the door. Stuff like that. Just great! And the two other guys seemed very happy about that. Definitely not two people I'd want to hang out with. And since they were the only other people on the floor, I just stuck to my room.

I couldn't get my Internet set up. My only distraction was my DVD player on my computer. So I watched lots of movies. *Harry Potter, Lord of the Rings, Chasing Amy*. It didn't help. The room felt so empty. Most of the stuff was Jade's, who still hadn't shown up. I couldn't make the room feel like my own. I didn't want to touch any of her stuff w/o her permission.

My stomach was tied up in knots. I wanted to be home so badly. I only left my room to go to the bathroom. I don't think I've ever been so lonely. Or so home-sick. I tried closing my eyes, and cuddled up with Mewie [my favorite stuffed cat], but I couldn't fall asleep. The room was too quiet. It felt so hollow. I ended up calling Mom, sobbing all over the place. We stayed on the phone for two hours. I almost fell asleep on the phone. I couldn't make myself say goodbye. I needed to hear her voice. It was one of the worst nights of my life.

As Mom always says, I don't know how to do this.

I really miss my mom!

CAROL Monday, September 2

Went to see Maggie today. Couldn't help myself. Brought her a rug for her room. After last night, I needed to know she was okay. She's fine, but I'm not. Can't even think about writing. I don't know how to do it without her.

MAGGIE September 2

I can't stand this. I still haven't met my roommate. This dorm is so noisy. I'm getting a headache. And I don't have any aspirin. The wind's whipping around the building, adding to the noise. And I have to share the shower with the whole floor. Never had to wait on line to take a shower. Grrr

Mom came up to bring me stuff from home. It was so good to see her. I think I can make it through another night.

CAROL Tuesday, September 3

Talked to Maggie three times today. This is almost as bad as withdrawing from alcohol. I suggested she switch her dorm. Now I have to drop it. But I *so* want to fix this for her!

MAGGIE September 3

I registered for classes. My schedule is great. And I finally met my roommate. I guess she seems okay. She doesn't say much. And she smokes, which is really bad. She asked me if I minded that she smoke in the room. Uh, yeah I mind. I said I'd rather she didn't. I found out where she's been the last two nights. At her boyfriend's dorm. So there's a plus. Hopefully she'll stay there a lot and won't need to smoke in our room.

I guess I'm getting the full college experience. Annoying roommate, crazy dorm, having to wait to take a shower...I wish I were home.

CAROL Wednesday, September 4

I called Ruth today. Rose started classes at Skidmore. Ruth is hurting as much as I am. Misery definitely loves company. I also called Rickey. He's hurting too. We're both so glad he got her that cell phone. Talked three more times today.

MAGGIE September 4

Classes started. And I got to all of them on time. Yay me. I love my Biology of Cancer and Aids class. Dr. Reiner rocks. But when I got back to my room, Jade and her boyfriend were there, getting high and playing video games.

So not cool. I felt so awkward, which is really unfair, 'cause it's my room too.

Except that since she's a sophomore, she gives me the feeling I'm a guest in the room. And she doesn't go to bed till 3:00am. Of course, the floor doesn't quiet down 'til then anyway, but it's easier to block out the noise outside the door than the noise inside. I just hope she crashes at her boyfriend's tonight.

It's been hours since she left, and the room still reeks of pot. I'm just thankful they aren't having sex here. That would be too much. God, it's hard enough getting used to being on my own w/o having to deal with this.

CAROL Thursday, September 5

Went up to see Maggie again. This is *worse* than alcohol withdrawal. Wonder if they have a 12-Step meeting for empty nesters!

MAGGIE September 5

I'm so glad Ann's in three of my classes. I just wish she didn't live way on the other side of campus. She says her roommate may be moving out. I'm thinking it might be a good idea to move in with her. Then I won't have to wait on line to take a damn shower! Shit. It would sure be nice to get to sleep before 3:00 am.

MAGGIE September 6

Mom picked me up at school today. It's so good to be back in my own bed, in my own room, with my very own TV to watch. I feel like I could sleep forever.

CAROL Friday, September 6

Maggie is excited about her classes. What a relief. Her "Techniques in Performance" class sounds like so much fun. Three hours of drama games on both Monday and Friday afternoons. What a way to start her first year. Glad she's home for the weekend. I want to lock her in her room and toss away the key.

MAGGIE September 8

I felt so dizzy before Mom brought me back to school. And my stomach was killing me again. Ack. I can't stand this. And to make things worse, this room smells like pot. And I still haven't met anyone on my floor. No one seems very friendly. I think they all know each other from last year. This really sucks. I have to get out of this place.

CAROL Sunday, September 8

It was hard dropping Maggie back at her dorm. I watched her walk away, then cried. Glad she wants to come home, but I think it makes it tough for both of us. How can I tell her she can't come home? Better call Ruth to see if she has any wisdom to pass on.

MAGGIE September 9

Ann's roommate is not moving out, but there's another spot available in a suite on the same floor. I've gotta hustle to get into it.

CAROL Monday, September 9

Had an appointment with Renee today and cried the whole session. Then drove up to UMass to take Maggie out to lunch. Will I ever be able to let her go?

MAGGIE September 10

I went down to Whitmore and filled out a form to move into McNamara, hopefully on Ann's floor. I should find out exactly where in the next couple of days. I don't think I'll have any problem getting in there. A lot of freshmen are moving out, because they want to be in 'party central.' Good news for me.

CAROL Tuesday, September 10

I talked to Rickey again. It's funny how we get along—now that we have nothing charged left between us. Sat at my computer and wrote a few pages of "Amelia and Bessie." It felt good to be writing again. I went for almost an hour without thinking about Maggie. Then called her three times tonight.

CAROL Wednesday, September 11

Called Sara at the library. We scheduled a poetry reading for October 17. Oh my gosh. My first big reading. Forty-five minutes of just my poetry. Yikes! I really hope Mag can come. Wow, we only talked twice today!

MAGGIE September 12

Yay. I got into McNamara. Same floor Ann's on, but a different suite. We'll be floor mates. I am so glad I'm getting out of this madhouse.

CAROL Thursday, September 12

Maggie is moving out of that crazy dorm she's in. Hallelujah. Len called. I'm seeing him in 2 weeks. Not sure how I feel about going away right now. There's a tug of war going on inside me.

MAGGIE September 14

Dad came up for a football game, Go Minutemen!, then helped me move my stuff over to McNamara. My new roommate's name is Lauren. She's a freshman too. Nursing major. Very sweet girl. As opposed to antisocial Jade. This definitely feels like a better situation. Everyone in the suite seems cool. And I like the whole setup. More privacy, but it's also easier to get to know people. Perfect combination. And I'll be sharing a bathroom with only seven girls, instead of twenty.

I think I'm starting to like college.

Like An Old Lover

I visit my daughter   fetch her at
her new address   a major university
where being seen with your mother
is against dorm rules. We cruise
into town open her first checking
account   as lack of funds is the
real reason for this sojourn. After
taking care of business   we settle
into ice cream   cramming down
grief with something sweet
always works for me.

And when I leave I realize that
seeing her now is like being with
an old lover   the one you gave
your heart and soul to   who has
just broken up with you   but still
wants to be friends   even though
you both know   it will never work.

Epilogue

CAROL   June 6, 2010

I'm happy to say, Maggie had a great first year in college. She loved all her classes and came home often, appreciating me far more for being away. Her following years at UMass had mixed reviews. In June of 2004, my 86-year-old mom took a bad fall in the parking lot of her retirement village in NJ. Our family shifted into crisis mode. Having to place her in a nursing home hundreds of miles away was heart-wrenching for all of us.

Earlier that year, Len's brother, Ed, finally succumbed to the wear and tear his weight put on his body. He died in January, only 57-years-old. My long-distance relationship with Len was crumbling and Maggie's dad was also struggling with his marriage to Teresa, eventually separating in December of that same year. All of these events seemed to take a toll on Maggie and her school work. I sensed she was mildly depressed, but after mentioning it once, I let it go, since my new MO was to zip the lips. She switched her major from theater to sociology in her junior year and graduated in 2006.

That year was filled with highs and lows for us. My picture book, *When the Cows Got Loose*, came out two months after Maggie graduated. In August, I put the house on the market, and that September, I got a call from Rickey. Maggie's stepmom, Teresa, who was staying at a hotel on Martha's Vineyard, was found dead in the prime of her life. The autopsy revealed she'd died from complications of anorexia and alcoholism. Maggie was devastated.

I attended the memorial service Rickey and Maggie planned. When asked if anyone wanted to come up and speak, I took a deep breath and walked to the front of the room, crowded with Rickey's and Teresa's friends. Taking another deep breath, I said I was not really one of Teresa's friends, that we'd certainly had our struggles, but I had come to love her through the heart of my daughter. As tears streamed down my face, I realized I had healed the wounds that were festering for years.

During this time, Rickey and I became friends again. He came to holidays at my sister's in Vermont, where my mom was in a nursing home after her fall. We felt like family again and even though I knew there was no chance of going back to what we once had, this was a new beginning for us, a fresh start, building bridges to something we could all live with.

MAGGIE

A lot has changed since I wrote that last journal entry. I graduated from college with a degree in sociology, quite a shift from my original plan to study theater. In the fall, I'll be starting grad school and will be on my way to becoming a social worker. I'm an adult and I finally feel like one, an idea that has been reiterated from re-reading my entries and feeling totally disconnected to the person I was in high school. Everything seemed so big then, so important. I know better now.

One of the biggest changes that occurred in my life in college was my relationship with my parents. I think my living away from home gave my mom and me the room to figure out how to interact with each other as adults. Not being in each other's space all the time helped ease tensions too. But I think even more so than with my mom, things changed with Dad and Teresa.

As I wrote in the journal, my relationship with my stepmother was often a difficult one. It's taken me years, but I think I finally understand why things were the way they were. Some of our difficulties, I think, were simply the result of Teresa not knowing how to parent a child and our jealousy towards each other over my dad's attention. When it was just the two of us, we actually got along really well and had a lot of fun. It was when we both had to compete for my dad's attention that things got messy. But that all changed my freshman year, when they separated. I knew it was coming (unlike my parent's split) because Teresa actually warned me she was struggling in the marriage.

I can clearly remember sitting on the front porch of Dad's house talking to her about it. Obviously I don't know everything that happened, but I do know how much older my dad was started to affect her. I don't think their 18 year age difference really mattered to her, until my dad turned 60. She told me she started panicking about how he would die long before her. She told me they might be separating, and they did.

And it's horrible to say, but it was the best thing for my dad's and my relationship. We would meet up in Northampton or Amherst for dinner every other week and talk about everything that was going on. I was finally able to be open with him about how much he hurt me in high school—how I felt pushed aside for Teresa. It was a healing of massive proportions. And Teresa also made the effort to keep up a friendship with me. She wanted me to know she was always there for me if I needed anything.

There are moments in life where everything slows down, and you realize that everything you know is about to change. I woke up at my mom's house on Sept 9, 2006 to find out my dad was downstairs. And everything slowed down. Teresa was dead.

****

From Maggie's Livejournal 9/9/06

Teresa died in her sleep last night. she was at martha's vineyard w/her sister and brother-in-law, and this morning they couldn't get her to wake up. my step-mother is dead at age forty-four.

i've gone through today in a total daze. teresa made my life hell for a significant portion of high school, but she was my family and i love her so much. love her...i guess it's loved now. oh god, i can't believe i have to use past tense. this is a nightmare. i keep waiting for it to end. My dad's in hamilton now making arrangements w/the rest of her family. i'm still unclear if the funeral's going to be there or here. last i spoke to dad, it sounds like we're going to have a ceremony here. but first there's going to be an autopsy. they're going to cut teresa up. and she hates needles. this can't be happening.

****

Teresa suffered heart failure as a result of alcoholism and anorexia. I knew she was really skinny the last time I saw her, but never in a million years could I have predicted this. Dad and I were in a daze. Mom was a rock for us; I don't know if I could have made it through that time without her support. No matter what kind of relationship I had had with Teresa, she was my stepmother, my family, who had been in my life for over ten years, and I loved her. And then she was gone. And I'll never have the chance to have the relationship I always wanted with her. It's incomplete.

It took me a long time to recover from losing Teresa. Her death has left me with an overactive fear regarding my mom and dad dying suddenly. I even get nervous when my mom oversleeps, and I feel compelled to check if she's okay. That's something I'm learning to live with. I do think I treasure my parents more, and I'm much more aware of the time I have with them. I spent years pushing, pushing, wanting to get away from them. And now that the cage door has been opened, I still linger, not quite ready to fly.

CAROL

Most of the manuscripts I mentioned in this memoir have yet to find publishers, but with the urging of my daughter, I began working on a memoir of my own in 2014, which eventually became *Stumbling Home: Life Before and After That Last Drink*, released by our publisher, Heliotrope Books, in 2021. It could be considered the prequel to *Wake Up, Maggie!*.

Acknowledgements

We'd like to thank the following people who supported us through the process of writing and publishing this book.

CAROL

First and foremost, my beloved daughter, Maggie, who unbeknownst to her, this memoir we started as a journal project when she was 15, would come to fruition 24 years later. This is her second memoir journey with me, putting up with all my angst the first time around for Stumbling Home, enduring hundreds of FaceTime calls and my ongoing anxiety. I am supremely grateful for her keen editorial eye, her sympathetic ear, and her loving support.

To my dear sister, Sui, who's always been my biggest cheerleader, who's read and offered praise and feedback on many of my early drafts since my writing days began. I value her opinion greatly; my brothers, John and Phil, whose goofiness always makes me laugh; Lauren and Joe, who held our hands through the college search. And my brother-in-law, Phil, whose love and hugs I will always miss.

To our Panama family: Matt, Becky, and Andrew, who along with my sister, have prayed for our success; Elyse and Izzy, who's creative photoshoot helped make our cover possible; and Mark, who has a sizable following on social media and who we'll count on to spread the word about the book with his sister on the cover. Hint, hint!

To my Jondreau family: Mary, Liz, Lorrie, Kathy, Tara, who all supported our early efforts;

Of course, I wouldn't be the writer I am today without the love and support of my writing group: Linda and Nancy, who listened to me read this in its early stages and didn't act bored, and for their artful eyes during our cover design: Tom, who always made me laugh and delivered valuable critique; and Elaine, who I miss.

A huge thank you to our dear publisher, Naomi Rosenblatt, who took another big chance on my second memoir, and whose kindness and patience with us is beyond measure. And our publicist, Jen Maguire, who jumped in and enthusiastically joined our *Wake Up, Maggie!* team.

I am eternally grateful to my therapist, Renée, who held my hand with compassionate eyes as I poured out my heart in our years of sessions, and who read an early draft of the first chapter, giving me the encouragement I needed to continue and recommendations that I used. And to Marcia, whose strong hands kneaded out the pain these years caused.

To Pennie, whose steadfast support got me through these challenging years in more ways than I can convey on this page, for which I will always be profoundly grateful.

To my friends: Belle, who has quelled my anxieties through this often stressful writing and publishing process; Trina, who gave us the working title, "Same Landscapes, Different Views," for our memoir, and who leaves the best voice messages cheering me on; Joanie; who read early drafts and suggested I censor some of the foul language (and believe it or not, we did); Leslie, who lent me her ear when I needed to talk. I cherish you all.

To Pat Stacey, who read the earliest version and took it on as our first editor, helping us make it into a readable memoir, and her sister, Paula, who helped me shape our book proposal.

To Caroline, who published my first essay about our project.

To Greg Joly, for *Divorce Papers*, and to Kevin Lewis, for *When the Cows Got Loose*.

To Maggie's dad, Rickey, who helped me bring our pride and joy into the world, and who after all we've been through, is still in my life. We've come a long way. For that I am grateful.

And finally, to those I may have forgotten, please forgive me. I love you all!

MAGGIE

Without my mom's determination and perseverance, this would not be a book. Even though she drove me crazy during this whole process, I am forever thankful to her for making me an author. I wish I had the words to express how grateful I am that you are my mom.

To Dad, for supporting me no matter what and for giving me the sister we never knew I had. You are my favorite person to have a conversation with.

To Aunt Susie and Uncle Phil, who came to every play and every concert and have always made me feel so loved. Uncle Phil, I'll miss you forever.

To Cait, for her decades of friendship and for making me the godmother to the sweetest, smartest, and funniest little girl I know. And to Pat, who always makes me laugh; both with him and at him.

To all my friends who got me through high school. You know who you are 'cause you're in this book.

To all my teachers, even the ones who made my time in high school miserable, I thank you for pushing me to be better.

Author Bio: Carol

Photo © 2021 Maggie Henley

CAROL WEIS is the author of the memoir *Stumbling Home: Life Before and After That Last Drink*, the Simon & Schuster children's book *When the Cows Got Loose*, and the poetry chapbook, *Divorce Papers*. Her writing has appeared in the New York Times, Washington Post, AARP, Cosmo, the Independent, Salon, ESPN, Ravishly, GH, Today's Parent, Literary Mama, Guideposts, and numerous other outlets, and has been read as commentary on NPR. A single Mom for 13 years, Carol is a Jersey girl who lives in Massachusetts, close to her grand kitties. You can follow her on Twitter, Facebook and Instagram. **carolweis.com**

Author Bio: Maggie

Photo © 2024 Maggie Henley

MARGARET HENLEY is the Clinical Director of a therapeutic group care program for children and adolescents. She received her Master's in Social Work from Westfield State University in 2014. She lives in Massachusetts with her fur babies, Wonton and Wasabi. *Wake Up, Maggie! Go Away, Mom!* is her debut memoir.

www.ingramcontent.com/pod-product-compliance
Lightning Source LLC
Chambersburg PA
CBHW032043080426
42733CB00006B/180